Avoid
Retirement
and
stay alive

David Bogan &
Keith Davies

Avoid
Retirement
and
stay alive

The New Retirement Revolution

New York   Chicago   San Francisco   Lisbon
London   Madrid   Mexico City   Milan   New Delhi
San Juan   Seoul   Singapore   Sydney   Toronto

The **McGraw·Hill** Companies

First published in New Zealand in 2007 by HarperCollins
Publishers (New Zealand) Ltd.
This edition published by arrangement with HarperCollins
Publishers (New Zealand) Ltd.

1 2 3 4 5 6 7 8 9 0   **FGR/FGR**   0 9 8 7

ISBN: 978-0-07-154593-8
MHID: 0-07-154593-X

McGraw-Hill books are available at special quantity discounts to use as
premiums and sales promotions, or for use in corporate training
programs. For more information, please write to the Director of Special
Sales, Professional Publishing, McGraw-Hill, Two Penn Plaza, New
York, NY 10121-2298. Or contact your local bookstore.

This book is printed on acid-free paper.

Contents

Acknowledgments

We have a number of professional and private debts. We began this book with a belief in a concept; a perception that only became a reality once we had explored it with people who were actually living it. For that we are particularly indebted to the inspirational Tina Hellesoe and Dr. Leslie Kay, along with the many other exceptional people who shared their life stories with us and remain anonymous to spare their blushes. Our research took us to numerous organizations and libraries around the world and to these very private toilers we express our sincere gratitude.

And

A very special thank you to Carrie Davies for her meticulous and tireless attention to detail and Mary Bogan for her enduring support.

What we're all about

This book is geared to change the lives of all who read it. It explores and explodes the myth of retirement, an insidious virus that has found its way into our subconscious and persuades us to act against our best interests. Our simple premise is that retirement is a fallacy—a notion to be banished from all sensible conversation.

In this book we promote the view that no one should feel compelled to retire; no one should want to retire. Yes, we may need to rearrange our lives to suit changing circumstances and requirements, but there is no room for the view that we should stop and vegetate. We have a single focus, a single message. A truly simple message, and never has a message been more timely:

Avoid retirement and stay alive.

Everyone seems to be in awe of the baby boomers, the generation born between 1946 and 1964, many of whom are now fast approaching the age of sixty-five. What will happen when they all retire? After all, one of America's

79 million baby boomers turns fifty every 7.5 seconds. In 2006 they began celebrating their sixtieth at the same rate; they're living longer and they know they have a problem. Three out of ten of those closest to retirement report having less than $10,000 in retirement savings, about enough for one small operation. And it's the same story the world over.

Coming right behind them are their children—rather like the second and third even more devastating waves of a tsunami—the Generation Xers and then the echo boomers. Fifty million Generation Xers were born in the sixties and seventies, closely followed by the echo boomers, born in the eighties and nineties, of whom there are a further 80 million.

They are the genetic offspring and demographic echo of their parents, the baby boomers; each and every one of them programmed to a life of ease and diminished responsibility, and already wondering how to carry that through into retirement.

And it doesn't end in America. Wherever you go in the Western world, they make up to a third of the population. In the United Kingdom there are more than 20 million people over the age of fifty. Even the tiniest of countries is affected, with New Zealand, at the bottom of the globe, facing the imminent prospect of 25 percent of its population being sixty-five years or older. The story is the same for its neighbor, Australia, with nearly 4.5 million baby boomers.

What makes these statistics truly frightening is that few of these countless millions have prepared themselves financially, physically, or emotionally to survive in retirement. Not only that, but thanks to improved diet, fitness, and medical care, their retirement will last for decades, not a few short years as was once the case.

> Retirement will last for decades, not a few short years as was once the case.

Millions of people are expected to stop work on a given day, without the financial wherewithal, and are now facing the stark reality that their respective governments probably don't have sufficient money in the bank to care for them.

Throughout the affluent West there are, quite literally, hundreds of millions of frightened people in their forties, fifties, and early sixties. Are you one of them? Frightened because you've been told that soon you must stop and retire, but you don't know how you will manage?

As problem, conflict, and crisis managers, we specialize in dealing with misconceptions. Most of the problems we deal with on a daily basis exist purely in the minds of our clients, and much of our focus is on changing attitudes and perceptions. Once you manage to do that, you'll usually find that the problem really does become an opportunity. This has always been well understood by the Chinese, who see a crisis as "an opportunity riding on a crest of a wave."

We initially met through a mutual client and have since combined our skills in media management and conflict resolution. The most common hurdle we've found in many years of working in these areas is getting clients to understand that "perception is reality," because often the simplest of realities is overlooked. We've had plenty of opportunities to test our ideas, and indeed we've been challenged to back them up at many public forums, including London University's Birkbeck College, Pepperdine, Harvard, and various MBA executive skills sessions. Our methods have stood the test of time, and we continue to assist our clients to solve communication-related issues by breaking the battle for hearts and minds into five essential requirements: perception, perception, perception, perception, and perception.

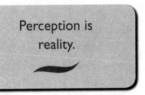

Perception is reality.

And what is it that we always seek to do for our clients, besides saving them money or face? To give them the skills to see into the heart of the crisis they find themselves in, and by doing so to also see the way out—to surf the wave of the opportunity rather than be submerged by it.

Surf the wave of the opportunity rather than be submerged by it.

So it is with retirement, in a world where upwards of 30 percent of the populations of most countries in the developed world are about to be confronted with this self-induced crisis. We know from many years of experience that most every crisis have a misconception at its core, so we set about looking for the misconception at the heart of the retirement issue, treating it as we would any other client crisis.

The bad news: there can be little doubt that retirement is a crisis in anyone's language. The good news: a crisis tends to grab

Most every crisis has a misconception at its core.

everyone's full, undivided attention, just as we hope we have your full and undivided attention by now. You may, of course, decide to dress it up as just a little emergency, but when you wake up in the morning it'll still be a crisis in an ill-fitting dress. We define a crisis as anything with the potential to cause lasting damage, and retirement does exactly that—it shatters lives. The answer is to develop a detailed crisis management plan, tailored to your specific needs, just as if you were a company in crisis.

The first step we always urge is to bring the situation under control. Attitude is everything here, and being positive beats being negative every time.

Attitude is everything.

The next thing we do is focus on protecting people first and property second. So it is with the retirement crisis. You need to organize your life and then your assets, to ensure you can happily work and live through the retirement years.

If you were a company the next few steps would be aimed at putting the media to bed, but you needn't worry about that. What you should do, though, is what the giant corporations do in order to deal with the ongoing effects of the crisis, which is gather the facts—who, what, where, when, why, how, and what next. This allows you to draw up your personal escape route from the crisis zone. Then, if necessary, activate your own crisis management team—this may include family and friends—who can all contribute ideas, support, and resources.

A crucial component of any crisis plan is being prepared, and retirement certainly isn't an unpredictable issue. You've known about it for years because you've had a lifetime of programming to volunteer yourself for this crisis of your own making. This actually makes it easier to be prepared, because the programming has already identified for you all the negative scenarios that *will* occur unless you take direct action.

> Crises won't go away just because you want them to.

Armed with all the facts and a positive attitude, the next active step in any crisis is to take responsibility for the safety and wellbeing of any victims, and in this case you're the potential victim. You may not see yourself as a victim, but you will very quickly become one if you're not careful. Don't try to minimize the seriousness of the situation—it won't go away just because you want it to.

In any volatile and confusing situation, it's essential to remain in control and be flexible. Be prepared to change, as only then can you maintain control of the situation. If you're inflexible, the crisis will probably overwhelm you.

And please, be honest. We've lost count of the number of crises that turned pear-shaped because someone failed to be honest. If you attempt to minimize the seriousness of the situation or mislead anyone, it's likely to blow up in your face. We're not talking about misleading the media or your staff or the stock exchange, we're talking about pulling the wool over your own eyes. You wouldn't credit how many people are prepared to do just that when it comes to retirement.

The good news is that there's an easy answer. Just banish the word "retirement" from your vocabulary. The following chapters will show you how.

> Banish the word "retirement" from your vocabulary.

In a nutshell

If you're being honest, do you feel a bit uneasy about the retirement dream? Well, relax—you're not alone. Your instincts are trying to tell you something and your instincts are right. Retirement isn't natural, and it certainly has no dream ending—anything but. For some people, retirement is their own personal living nightmare. The notion of retirement itself is a fallacy, a virus-like concept that will take over and control your life, a dangerous notion to be excluded from all sensible conversation.

If you disagree with that last sentence, then the "retirement virus" has already hijacked your brain into believing retirement is good for you. To get it back, you have to allow your inbuilt anti-virus program—your intuition—to act.

As of now you have permission to eradicate "retirement" from your vocabulary. Delete it from

> Delete "retirement" from the software of your mind, drag it kicking and screaming into the trash.

the software of your mind, drag it kicking and screaming into the trash. That's it. Retirement gone forever.

Never mention the dreaded word again. It simply isn't going to happen; instead you're going to keep on living. And if you have any lingering doubt about why we're telling you this, then consider the definition of the word retirement—*to remove from view; withdraw from society*. Do we need to say more?

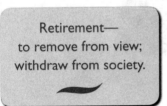

Retirement—
to remove from view;
withdraw from society.

Now you can start doing everything you have been putting off for later. What's more, you'll start to manage your time, your money and your life more sensibly, and before long you'll be delighted to find you have more of a life. We'll show you how.

We can hear you groaning now. A book telling you *not* to retire! What a load of nonsense that has to be. You've worked hard all your life and now you want to have some fun and enjoy yourself while you still can. You want to sit on the porch and read a book. Take a cruise. Play golf. See more of the family. Relax a little. Travel. Meet up with friends. Learn to paint. See the Great Wall of China. Socialize . . .

Excuse us for interrupting such an exciting train of thought, but you seem to be missing the point.

⌒ You have to retire to read a book?

⌒ You have to retire to see more of your family?

⌒ You have to retire to travel?

In short, you seem to be telling us you need to retire to get a life. For your own sake, stop and think about that for a moment. If you accept that argument, then you've bought into the ridiculous notion that retirement is to be longed for, something desirable.

Right now you may feel tired, and you probably are, but all you need to do is take a rest or maybe change your life a little. But termination? Surely not.

Before you do another thing, let's take a look at a typical retired person. There's a very good chance you're looking at someone who has read a book, taken a trip, patted the grandkids on the head, and is now sitting there waiting to gracefully fade away. Great. Fantastic. Just what you've worked all your life for. Yeah, right.

One of our more enlightened universities ran an experiment with its students, confronting them with a flash card list of positive words, a list that included "retirement."

The moment these healthy, energetic, and hopeful young things glimpsed the word "retirement" their blood pressure dropped, their heart rate lowered, and their shoulders visibly drooped. And they only saw the word for a fraction of a second.

There's an old saying "use it or lose it," and it applies to everything we do, both mental and physical.

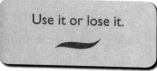

Use it or lose it.

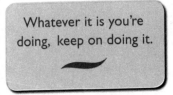

Whatever it is you're doing, keep on doing it.

Quite simply, this is the key message of our book. Whatever it is you're doing, keep on doing it.

Oh, we can hear you now. "But I *have* to retire, don't I?"

Well, you can certainly be forgiven for thinking so, but the answer is no. A resounding NO. Sure, you may not be able to carry on doing exactly what you're doing now, but to suggest you suddenly become worthless on a fixed date is totally ludicrous.

Think about this for a moment—ever noticed that those who can afford to retire, don't? More to the point, how many rich and successful men and women do you know who have retired and now do nothing?

Ever noticed that those who can afford to retire, don't?

It's a short list, and the reason for that is simple. Successful people love what they do—they have a passion, and because real passion never goes away, they never stop. One occupation may end, but they merely adapt, diversify, and continue. That's the trick.

Shortly, we'll introduce you to some down-to-earth yet truly successful men and women who have defied the retirement message. While thanking them for making time to share their experiences, we have taken the liberty of changing their names, and subtly disguising their stories to protect their anonymity, but we trust you will find their insights inspiring.

Of course, as you get older you have to get smarter to beat the system that pre-programs you to believe you must retire. We're programmed for the nightmare of retirement from the day we start our first job, and part of that programming even has us actively planning for that momentous day when we finish work. That's what society does to each and every one of us —consigns us to a living death.

> We're programmed for the nightmare of retirement from the day we start our first job.

We are conditioned to believe that on a certain date our lives will cease to have meaning, and we will become valueless. When that day comes we'll be ordered to stop, and we'll obey. How dare they!

There's a worldwide debate centred on the right to practice euthanasia, and whether or not doctors should be allowed to play God. In most countries, exceptional circumstances aside, we have determined not to allow doctors to administer a fatal dose or switch off life support. So why on earth would we allow anyone else to effectively end our lives by forcing us into retirement?

More to the point, why are any of us so silly as to go along with this abject nonsense? We go along with it because of that dreadful, self-imposed programming. We have been conditioned to believe that this is the way it should be; the way it's always been. And that's simply not true.

There is absolutely nothing in your genetic make-up to suggest the slightest desire to surrender. Quite the reverse—your very being revolves around a drive to live and play an active part within your community, and survive in a sustainable society.

You may not realize it, but this retirement business is relatively new, and we use the term "business" advisedly.

> You may not realize it, but this retirement business is relatively new.

As we shall see, retirement was dreamed up as a means of putting us out to pasture, to make way for younger and stronger recruits, in effect a means of ridding society of those who had rather inconveniently grown old. The same society that had geared its education system to ensure a sufficient number of students failed in order to guarantee a steady stream of unqualified manual labourers, was taking care of the ageing bulge at the other end of the industrial scale.

Now, in one of life's ironic little twists, the falling birth rate in Western societies today means there are fewer new workers, making a nonsense of the original rationale for retirement.

Can you do something about it? Can you get your life back? Is it too late? You most certainly can, and it's never too late. For a start you can forget all that retirement nonsense, but you're going to have to keep your wits about you and be extra positive. All around you there are people preaching the retirement message and, worse still, retiring.

A leading newspaper ran a retirement supplement with the headline "You're never too young to start saving." And to drive the point home, they featured a child in diapers surrounded by piles of dollar bills. A baby thinking of retirement! This "one-stop shop for planning retirement" appeared with an accompanying article about a trust organization fronted by two thirty-year-olds. With a heading, "Age wave about to strike," it warned that people born at the beginning of the baby boom in 1946 would soon hit sixty years of age and be heading into retirement, with "serious implications for several countries." Also preaching that it was never too soon to start saving, it pointed out that only 17 percent of men and 7 percent of women over the age of sixty-five were in full-time employment. And just what did all these key messages have in common? Fear, and a desire to part you from both your independence and your money.

They are shock tactics designed to make you fearful about your future and convince you to put your faith, and money, of course, with someone younger who will look after it for you—as if youth was ever a criterion for safer investing. If they are so good, you might care to ask, why aren't they busy investing their own money?

> Shock tactics are designed to make you fearful about your future.

The sole intention is to remove your independent thought processes and have you buy into the retirement nightmare that only "they" can help you with. By "help," they mean taking an upfront slice of your savings as a management fee, before investing what's left, leaving you to take all the risk. Doesn't sound like much of a deal.

> You do not have a sign stamped on your forehead that reads, "Best before sixty."

The simple truth is you do *not* have a sign stamped on your forehead that reads, "Best before sixty (or sixty-five or even seventy-five)." So why on earth behave as though you do? The silly notion of a *use-by* date is all part of the fallacy we have accepted of retirement being our predestined fate. After all, *use by* is a euphemism for "throw out after this date." Accept the retirement label and you are subconsciously accepting that the "best" of life has passed you by. Nothing really matters anymore, and nothing in life will ever be as good again.

What a load of rubbish, yet we're all conditioned to accept it as a reality. And the moment you accept it, the moment you resign yourself to retirement—the slow death begins. Your imagination starts confusing fact with fiction and romantic idealism with reality. Buy into the notion that retirement is somehow a desirable outcome and, before you can scream "help," life has no greater challenge than to sit around in God's waiting room. Heaven forbid!

You need to remind yourself that you belong to a generation that is fitter and healthier than any before. In all likelihood, you have the same energy and drive you had twenty, even thirty years ago. You are no more worn out and ready for the scrap heap than you were then. Why on earth would you want to waste such tremendous assets—which includes a lifetime of experience—by retiring?

And continuing to work is now a real option. The facts speak for themselves. Throughout the Western world there is a hunger for talented and experienced people. Survey after survey shows that growing numbers of employers *want* to retain their older employees. Perhaps that should have read *need* to retain their older employees.

Proof of how serious this has become can be found in Russia, where the population is dropping by 700,000 people a year. This information has been classified, by a government usually not overly keen on confessing its nation's shortcomings in public, as "the most acute problem facing modern Russia." And with this dire warning came the suggestion of paying baby bonuses to encourage couples to help solve the problem.

This is a worldwide issue, and with it has come a realization that people in their fifties, sixties, and over are rather useful to have around. With all the labor-saving devices now available, and the fact that we live in an age dominated by ease and speed of access to information, there is no physical reason why you can't keep going for as long as you like.

Besides, you're used to the good things in life. Why on earth would you want to scrimp and save for the occasional treat when you can carry on receiving your just rewards by working at least part-time? And the part-time option should be your decision, not someone else's, just as you can make the call to take on a less stressful or high-powered job. More of that later.

How were we so misled? How could the Western world have got it so wrong? North America, Europe, Great Britain, and Australasia have all locked themselves into the self-destructive mania of retirement, with a conviction that it was all for the betterment of mankind.

Pensions and retirement are quite modern phenomena. For most of human history people didn't retire, they worked and died. It wasn't as bad as it sounds. People assumed they would live useful lives; in fact, they took it for granted, and their community valued them. Their age and wisdom were considered assets, as were the tasks they often performed in their later years.

> Give up your job by all means, but don't stop working.

Then came the switch from farm to factory and everything changed. Overnight, age became a liability. A worker's sole asset in the factory was their strength; when that diminished, no one was interested in how wise they might be. After all, they weren't employed for their wisdom. Quite the reverse in fact, and retirement became a beckoning light at the end of the tunnel. Rather like the fires the shipwreckers of old lit to attract unsuspecting ships onto rocky shorelines.

There was a further problem. By the 1930s a worldwide depression was in full swing and unemployment soared. Governments struggled to cope with idle young men roaming the countryside in search of work, while older workers hung on to their jobs for dear life.

Notice that word. *Job*. It takes up just one line in the dictionary—*a piece of work, usually done for hire or a profit*. And there's the rub. A job is usually something we do to make someone else a profit.

Work, on the other hand, is quite a different matter. "Work" is a word the dictionary writers can wax lyrical about for pages. It can be succinctly put—*expenditure of energy, striving, application of exertion for a purpose*. Note the crucial difference—for a purpose. One is for "profit" and the other for a "purpose."

Put simply:

Job = profit = money
Work = purpose = life-engaging

That word *purpose* may or may not have money-making at its heart. It may entail, and frequently does, little more than the sheer pleasure of it all. Working is an integral part of life's purpose, a function for which we are genetically "hard-wired," part of our essential survival kit. So, give up your job by all means, but don't stop working. Jobs come and go. Work is the constant.

The "system" encourages all and sundry to have a job and throws in the bait of retirement, dressed up as that Old Testament-style offer of the promised land— endless leisure—cleverly designed to make all the years of productive drudgery appear worthwhile. The company pension plans, the state handouts, the glossy brochures are all designed to reassure you that you're on the right path, a glimpse of the land of milk and honey that lies ahead. Just a bit more drudgery, just a bit more, and it will all be worth it. Are you starting to get the picture?

"Social security" became the buzzword as leaders everywhere pompously proclaimed their belief in social justice and welfare for all. There was never any talk of how it would all be paid for, just endless promises. Trust us, vote for us, and we'll look after you. Soon a form of institutionalized retirement was in place from America to Great Britain to Europe and Australasia. Now the pressure was really on for people to retire with the bait of a state handout. And it worked.

People began retiring earlier and earlier, usually after reading retirement brochures full of happy, smiling young people lounging around country clubs. Now there were company retirement pensions on top of social security benefits that were in turn linked to cost-of-living increases. Life really couldn't get any better.

Retirement had been cleverly and subtly branded with an impeccable and highly desirable image of health, wealth and happiness. How does the saying go? If it sounds too good to be true, then it probably is.

> If it sounds too good to be true, then it probably is.

Those who retired early were practically driven crazy by the futility of their wonderful new lives. They'd taken on board the healthy food and exercise message, preached by the very same marketers now peddling the retirement dream. Credit where credit is due, though, they did at least get that one right, with unfortunate side effects. Thanks to much improved medical care and a healthier lifestyle, the new retirees were now fit enough to run marathons, not sit around being useless.

There was worse to come as the best-laid political plans started to unravel. The falling birth rate meant a reduced workforce, which in turn meant a smaller tax take and less money to support the idyllic country club lifestyle of the retirement brochures. The world began waking up to the reality that retirement isn't what it's made out to be. Not that our leaders have cottoned on to the actual problem yet. Absorbed in dealing with the hugely negative effects, they've overlooked the cause.

In April 2005, President George W. Bush, talking about pension schemes, stated the obvious: "By 2041 the entire

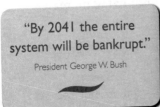

"By 2041 the entire system will be bankrupt."

President George W. Bush

system will be bankrupt." He proposed raising the retirement age from sixty-five to sixty-seven and could see it rising still further to seventy.

And it isn't just American presidents who see the writing on the wall. Governments the world over are struggling with the very same problem, a problem of their own creation.

To understand how we were so effectively conditioned for retirement in the first place, you have to understand how your intuitive brain relates to your rational brain.

Your brain is divided into several compartments with specific tasks and responsibilities. Here we are interested in just two—your intuitive brain and your rational brain. Put simply, your intuitive brain is the section that enables you to "know," while your rational brain enables you to "think."

Your intuitive brain is primed from conception to ensure your personal survival. Your DNA is programmed with a

Live; do anything you need to do to be safe and survive.

simple message which underpins your entire genetic coding: "Live; do anything you need to do to be safe and survive." The intuitive section of your brain is a truly special gift; it is your own uniquely truthful sounding-board for what is right and wrong *for you*.

Several hundred years ago, a rather wise gentleman by the name of Descartes wrote, *Cogito ergo sum*—I *think*, therefore I am. Had the venerable philosopher been aware of precisely how our brains manage data, he would have written *Cognito ergo sum*—I *know*, therefore I am. Because it is the *knowing* of your intuitive brain that drives and manages the *thinking* of your rational brain. Hence those tried and true phrases—*it suddenly dawned on me* and *the lights came on*, because that's what happens when your intuitive brain engages.

That brings us to the rational brain, which is something very different. Your rational brain deals in black and white—words—and is where your rational thoughts come from. You should treat the rational brain with great respect. For a start, it develops later and then, after some years in the sun, starts to fade away.

But there's worse to come—it's highly susceptible to outside programming. The rational brain's decision-making processes are easily taken over by external forces. Institutions from political to commercial to religious are expert at planting rational thoughts in our minds; thoughts paraded and disguised as intuitive brain thoughts that we buy into, believing them to be in our best interests. It's why you buy one car over another, and why you vote for one politician over another. And, of course, it's why you think retirement is a good idea.

The relationship between rational and intuitive thought is the subject of endless philosophical and scientific debate. In truth, nothing illustrates the inter-relationship better than those businesses pushing retirement schemes. Schemes we *buy* into, even though we are naturally programmed to survive, not retire. But, and this is the scary bit, with the right pitch our rational brain can manage to override our intuition or better instincts.

> Everything about the retirement concept is wrong.

Think about it for a moment. Everything about the retirement concept is wrong. We are *not* here to shrivel up on a given date and wait to die; your own instincts will tell you that, yet somehow we have been convinced otherwise.

That's why we suggested back at the beginning that you need to hit that delete button and rid yourself of the false concept of retirement. Our single goal in writing this book is to enable you to delete this insidious virus from your system, remove "retirement" from your vocabulary, and get your life back.

> Remove "retirement" from your vocabulary, and get your life back.

We'll expand on all these thoughts throughout the book, but in the meantime consider this. There is no greater manifestation of retirement shrinkage than the final new car. You know the one. The little car that will "see you out." And for goodness sake don't go anywhere in the new little car. You never know, it might not "see you out."

Sound scary? Can you believe people actually do this to themselves? Well, they do—like moths to the flame. The new little car subconsciously becomes a mobile coffin, and every time the proud new owner sits in it, they'll be thinking: "This is it, my last car ever, I only hope it will see me out." Is that you? Are you planning to be the proud new owner of a little car to see you out? Please tell us you aren't.

The next biggest mistake for self-imposed retirees, after buying the little car, is to move out to the beach, the country, a distant suburb, or small town. They want to "get away from it all."

What they don't realize is that we should "get away" only when we're stressed. As our stress levels drop, we need to be back where the action is, where we can fulfil our destiny of a full life. Live where the action is and stay in your community, be part of it, young and old, rich and poor, good and bad. That's life. We're all hardwired to be part of this intrinsic fabric, that's where we belong, being useful to ourselves and others.

> Live where the action is and stay in your community.

But how? This is a very good question that cuts to the heart of everything we are talking about. The question itself presumes that by now you have some healthy doubts about retirement; doubts about jumping or being thrown off the moving train, about vegetating and being useless. Good. Now you can consider a real future.

In the pages ahead we'll show you how to develop an action plan, a template for all ages and all backgrounds that you can customize into your own personal "golden parachute."

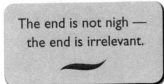

The end is not nigh — the end is irrelevant.

The end is not nigh—the end is irrelevant. What is important is to live life to the full, every day. This is nothing new; the philosophers have been saying it for years. What is new is that governments the world over have at long last realized they have a tiger by the tail, and are wondering what *they* should do with *our* lives.

The system, both public and private, is teetering on bankruptcy, and the snake oil salesmen are lining up to offer fresh promises, with "new" solutions that include retiring a few years later or raising taxes, or the truly generous offer to pay more, if you collect later, in the transparent hope you will conveniently die before payday. The list goes on.

Refuse to buy into any of this and listen to your intuition; after all, it's personalized for your safety and survival. Your life is *your* responsibility, so take it back. If you can trash the very concept of retirement you'll make a wonderfully positive start, and the following chapters will set you free. Learn how to liberate yourself from the misery of retirement and spell out what deep down you already know.

Your life is *your* responsibility, so take it back.

As our old friend Albert Einstein put it: "Your imagination is your preview of life's coming attractions."

This is it. Your life as it should be. Enjoy the ride.

Key points
to remember

✓ Retirement isn't natural—it was invented to solve an oversupply of labor

✓ You are genetically hard-wired to strive to keep alive

✓ You do not have a use-by date

✓ Society can't afford the retirement we all thought we were working for

2

But I have to retire —don't I?

Have you ever heard anything quite so silly? If you really want to know how ridiculous the whole idea of retirement is, ask yourself how many truly rich and successful people retire. Do you seriously think that when Bill Gates and Warren Buffett take an hour off to play bridge together they waste time chewing over their retirement options? Do the two richest men in the world dream of the day they'll be able to do nothing? Do they bore each other with talk of how wonderful it would be to spend lazy days by the pool, stirring occasionally for a round of golf? Of course not. And isn't that the great irony? Those who can afford to retire, don't. And those who can't, do.

> Those who can afford to retire, don't.

In short, they retain control of their lives, with a determination to survive.

Well, we're here to provide a survival guide for anyone foolish enough to contemplate retirement. Because if you *are* thinking about it, you've accepted the idea that since you were born you've been marking time before you enter the dock for society to pronounce sentence:

"You have been found guilty of working hard all your life. You will now pay for that. You are sentenced to live out the rest of your days in a truly worthless existence. We'll find you a little box to call home, where you will be expected to do less and eat less. And if you get sick we'll soak up any savings you might have, then put you at the back of the queue, behind all the other old and worthless people."

Because, quite simply, that's what society is trying to do to each and every one of us—consign us to a living death. If you didn't know better you'd swear it was a scene from a science fiction movie, complete with ominous music, about a future in which machines take over and control the human condition. And control is the only word for it—but we're the ones imposing this madness on ourselves, not evil machines. We've been socially programmed to accept the idea of retirement from the very first day we start work. It's been part of a deal we willingly buy into and grasp with both hands but—and this is the truly scary bit—we happily anticipate our retirement.

We accept that society has a right to tell us when to stop and willingly obey the order when it comes. Then to make sure we lose all sense of self-respect, we'll be palmed off with a pittance of a pension—enough to get by on if we're lucky. Just so long as we aren't planning to live anything that might resemble a life.

You might ask yourself why anyone would be silly enough to go along with this. The good news is that nowadays not everyone *is* going along with it and increasing numbers of people are rejecting the notion of retirement.

Richard didn't even consider it. An innovative engineer, his great skill was in people management. He rose to the top of two of the world's great appliance manufacturing and transport companies. Whenever or wherever there was a problem Richard always looked to himself. No one else was ever to blame. He became renowned for his favorite saying: "If you have a union problem, then you have a management problem; if you have a manufacturing problem, then you have a management problem; and if you have a customer problem, you inevitably have a management problem."

He never fired anyone for making a mistake, living by the motto: "The person who never made a mistake, never achieved anything."

Richard no longer runs companies, but he's forever jetting off to international board meetings at which his wisdom and experience are valued. There have been occasions when his raised eyebrow has been sufficient for an entire board and senior management team to drop a proposal they'd been supporting for months.

Richard brings experience to the table, and nothing beats experience. Been there, done that, made that mistake and learned from it. Needless to say he worked into his seventies and is still in demand. Smart companies keep people on long after their retirement age—after all, the alternative is to force them aside for what are certainly less experienced and often less able people.

Not that Richard spends all his life on planes or at meetings—he also has a life. To celebrate his eightieth birthday, this keen sailor launched a new ocean-going yacht and invited all his friends. It's worth noting here that many of those friends were much younger. Before inviting his wife of sixty years to break a champagne bottle across the bow of his new pride and joy, Richard made a typically short speech: "It was this or a retirement home."

And with that the yacht was launched, the party continued, and they sailed away on the maiden voyage.

OK, so we can't all jet about the world or buy fancy yachts, but we can all learn from Richard. Retirement effectively means out of sight and out of mind. If Richard had bought a retirement home rather than the yacht, would those same companies still want him on their board? The phone would have stopped ringing before you could say "house warming."

Effectively, that's what happens when we retire. We vanish, disappear from view and cease to exist, let alone have any value so far as the rest of the world is concerned, yet everywhere we look there is the promise—"Early retirement can be yours."

There are endless articles and advertisements telling you how to invest your money and save. You're urged to sign up immediately and stash away as much cash as possible so you have something worthwhile to invest. And the younger you are, the more adventurous you are encouraged to be—for *adventurous*, read *risky*. And don't worry about market turbulence; it's all part of the exciting journey towards that retirement dream. Better still, take real risk and that most electrifying of goals—an "early retirement"—could be yours!

The sheer nonsense of all this defies belief.

Thanks to better health care, better diet and exercise, we already face the prospect of spending nearly as much time in retirement

> Why do you think your expenses will decrease in retirement?

as we spend working. And now a bunch of young—you can be sure they are *very* young—financial planners are suggesting we consign ourselves to purgatory even earlier!

Government pension and welfare schemes the world over were initially developed with the confident expectation that most people would struggle to make it past retirement. Well, government got it wrong. It gets worse of course, but you've probably worked that out for yourself by now. We'll take a longer, more in-depth look at this later, but there was a time, not so long ago, when few, if any of us, lived long enough to retire.

A hundred years ago, the average life expectancy of a fit and able person living in the developed world wasn't much more than sixty years.

The sad reality was that most people worked until they became too sick or frail to continue; then, without the benefit of today's advanced medical knowledge and resources, they died. They were lucky to have a few miserable years of "retirement," whereas today many of us can expect to spend upwards of a third of our lives in the "retirement zone."

> Many of us can expect to spend upwards of a third of our lives in the "retirement zone."

Thanks to our improved health care and general wellbeing, we're living longer, but there are fewer youngsters coming up behind to support us. Not to worry, there are always those great returns to be had from the stock market. Trouble is, more and more of us are opting for the safety of boring old "term investments" offered by the banks, a development likely to cause lasting, if not terminal damage to the stock market. In short, plenty of capital is being invested but for limited, if somewhat safer, returns.

Ah well, not to worry, you can always sell the house. But who's going to buy your house, given all your neighbors might have the same idea? And for how much? For reasons we will expand on later, the "experts" are telling us to expect a massive, worldwide slump in house prices within this decade. Admit it, the thought had crossed your minds: sell the house and live off the profit. Well, that may be just another part of the dream waiting to turn into a nightmare. Much the same prediction is being made for the stock market, when the baby boomers decide to off-load their shares.

But wait, there's more. Many countries are finding that debt for the elderly is going up, not down. Two headlines from the British press say it all—"Millions still pay mortgage well into retirement" and "Age shall not wither power to raise cash."

Not to worry, the financial advisers and planners will tell you that on retirement you'll need only 70 percent of your pre-retirement income. What a load of nonsense.

For a start your medical and insurance bills will go through the roof, and unless you're planning a starvation diet your food bills will be the same, and quite possibly increase as friends and family descend on you more often.

You'll turn the light on just as frequently, continue to wear clothes and want to travel, possibly even more than when you were in full-time employment. Every additional activity to fill all that spare time will involve additional cost without the support of a corresponding increase in income.

Starting to get the picture? We'd like to see financial planners and retirement experts have *their* income slashed by 30 percent and try to maintain anything like their current standard of living.

On the other hand, they probably imagine you sitting around in the dark, wearing the same old clothes, existing on one meal a day in a state of perpetual prayer that your health holds out. And as for today's dollar being worth a fraction of its current value in a few years' time, don't worry, the ever-faithful financial planners will arrange your investments. Of course, getting the sort of return you'll need to keep you ahead of the game will entail a degree of risk. By now you might be getting an inkling of why they like to take their fees upfront.

So, where is this taking us? It's fine for the likes of Richard — financially well-off and successful — to carry on going to board meetings, but what about the rest of us? Do we have any other options?

Of course we do, but first we need to address the question itself — or, more to the point, the thinking behind it. You ask about options out of fear. No need to be embarrassed about that, it's quite natural to be afraid when you think about retirement; after all, we're all nervous about the unnatural and the unknown.

> "The trouble with retirement is you never get a day off."
>
> Abe Lemons, basketball coach,

Fortunately, fear only comes into the equation if you buy into the nonsense that at a given age you suddenly become worthless. If you can grasp the essential message of this book, that retirement isn't on the agenda and you're going to keep on living a worthwhile life, there's nothing to be afraid of—and you might even have the occasional laugh.

> "Retirement kills more people than hard work ever did."
>
> Malcolm Forbes

And you're going to need your sense of humor. Check out the number of shrinks making a living from treating retired people suffering from depression. Beating depression after retirement has become a growth industry as people who have stopped working often struggle to come to terms with the emptiness and despair that soon pervades their lives. Many lose their sense of purpose and self-esteem, with the most vulnerable being those who were previously the most successful. Once they were admired and

> "Retirement is the ugliest word in the language."
>
> Ernest Hemingway

looked up to on a daily basis and now, at a stroke, they're not. Yesterday they were fulfilling a significant role at work, in society, and within their families. Overnight they have lost all their "value." That's not true of course, but it's how they feel. Perception is reality and their self-perception is at the bottom of the barrel — both empty and rejected, and all because they've been conditioned to believe they *have* to retire, now that their *useful* lives have come to an end.

And yet . . .

Despite the fact that retirement is now big business, there are increasingly common examples demonstrating that retirement is an outdated notion.

Faced with skill shortages, many businesses are starting to realize the answer lies in an older workforce. Nowhere was this more graphically illustrated than in an ironic twist to the aftermath of the September 11 attack on the twin towers in New York. Tracking down the perpetrators required experienced operators, but the FBI had to concede that some 40 percent of its agents weren't up to the task. And what was the problem? They had five years or less experience. Sure, they could run fast, do endless push-ups and shoot straight, but when it came to experience they didn't have enough. As this was a national emergency the FBI bit the bullet and re-hired agents who'd been forced into retirement at fifty-seven. Look out bin Laden, here comes the gray brigade!

Since then, the U.S. Department of Labor has been forced to confront the implications of the stark reality that some 11,000 Americans turn fifty every day, many of them skilled workers who will be lost to the workforce, threatening both individual businesses and the overall economy. The answer lies in following the example of the FBI—keeping the brains, institutional knowledge and skill in-house, while at the same time recognizing that extensive worldwide research shows that the vast majority of people approaching retirement age are keen to continue working, albeit on a part-time basis.

Companies that were a bit quicker on the uptake and put this into practice are already reporting improved performance. The older workforce, far from being a liability, instead contributes to increased productivity and profitability. It's true that senior employees in general are slightly slower to pick up on new technology than their younger colleagues, but once they've picked it up, they tend to apply it more productively and with less error. And when it comes to that all-important work ethic and promptness, not to mention the old-fashioned notion of customer service, they're streets ahead. In fact, the majority of customers prefer dealing with older people and the truly smart companies now recognize the need to make their "senior" workers welcome and happy. Slowly the message is starting to dawn, but you can't afford to sit around waiting for the world to change. You're going to have to take the giant step yourself.

> You're going to have to take the giant step yourself.

Attitude is the name of the game, and all it really takes is for you to make that crucial mind change.

That's exactly what Angela did.

Approaching her retirement years, Angela faced a series of crises that would have brought lesser beings to their knees. Peter, her beloved husband of thirty years, had been struck down by cancer within weeks of their daughter being killed by a drunken driver in a horrific head-on crash. To cap it all off, Angela found herself on the scrap heap, victim of a mass lay-off at the accountancy firm where she'd flourished as the new business manager for the previous fifteen years.

Her friends kindly reminded her she was probably unemployable, a view quickly endorsed by the various agencies she approached. The best advice seemed to be: sell the family home, buy a one-bedroom apartment and live off the combined interest from what was left from the sale and her existing savings.

Angela was having none of that. Within two months the inheritance had gone. The family home now had a new side entrance, and two former bedrooms had been converted into a reception area leading into a suite any executive would have been proud of, equipped with the latest technology.

Angela was in business, offering a specialist marketing and business promotion service to small companies in her community, businesses that would normally never be able to afford the attention of such an experienced executive. She didn't sell herself cheap. For a start she didn't want to undervalue the advice she gave, yet knew it was important not to price herself out of the niche market she had created. Angela set about educating clients to use her sparingly, and, in the process, made herself a valued supplier who came highly recommended. Her reputation spread through word of mouth, and what began fifteen years ago has developed into a flourishing business with seventy-year-old Angela still at the helm.

Angela is living proof that you really don't have to retire. She might not be a Bill Gates or Warren Buffett, but she shares one all-important quality with them—she recognizes that retirement is a fallacy. And that's what you should be doing. Right now.

Key points to remember

✓ Those who can afford to retire, don't. And those who can't, do

✓ Nothing beats experience, and forward-looking companies are beginning to recognize this

✓ Your expenses don't decrease after retirement

✓ Economically and socially, retirement is an outdated concept

3

The retirement boom goes bust

Retirement is the biggest system failure in the Western world. Millions of people have accepted a false notion and spent a great chunk of their lives dealing with the consequences, resulting in epidemics of depression and anxiety.

> Retirement is the biggest system failure in the Western world.

How did we get it so wrong?

As we have seen, retirement is a relatively modern phenomenon. Young people who had been expected to support their ageing parents flocked to the towns and cities to provide labor for those dark satanic mills and factories.

Unfortunately, by the 1930s there was that worldwide depression. One solution that was widely accepted was to influence older workers to step aside for younger and fitter ones. Enter the retirement package, stage left.

Institutionalized retirement became the norm with the bait of a state handout. And it worked. People remained productive and worked for the retirement dream at the "end of their working lives," just like a donkey follows a carrot on a stick. The catch in our case was that the system, not the worker, determined where the end of the road lay and made asses of us all.

Once workers slowed down and became less agile and strong they effectively lost their premium assets. Judged less able to keep up physically and mentally, they were dispatched to the retirement pool in God's waiting room to make way for younger and quicker hands.

Retirement was then rebranded with an image of health, wealth, and happiness. Life would be one long holiday after an eternity at the grindstone. Bring it on, we cried—the sooner the better. We realize we're recapping here but it really does bear repeating.

Everything would have been fine, except people began to ask for more. Not only that, they began retiring earlier and living longer and, even worse, began asserting their independence. How ungrateful was that?

Over-sixties used to live with their children or other relatives—today only a tiny fraction of the "elderly" live with their families. From once relying on, and being dependent upon, their increasingly unreliable children, the new retirees looked forward to self-financed independence and leisure. Why?

Simple. Their ungrateful children, who were being educated in ever-growing numbers, had skills and knowledge that were in high demand in the mushrooming industrial hinterland of the cities. In ever-increasing numbers they left home with no inclination to return and look after their geriatric parents. After a generation or two the message dawned—having children wasn't the answer. The answer lay in having *less* of those expensive offspring and saving their money for their old age.

Over time it became even easier; an improved education system created a vastly improved standard of living, with the average Westerner now some eight times better off than his or her forbears of a century ago. This made it significantly easier for them to save for retirement.

And because governments had moved into the retirement game, the pressure went on to raise more taxes to pay for the ever-increasing number of people putting out their hand for a ticket to the land of retirement bliss. The words "financial crisis" were soon being heard from London to Washington to Paris to Tokyo to Sydney to Auckland. Everywhere, the growing and ageing population was becoming increasingly and desperately dependent on a shrinking workforce, all compounded by a declining birth rate.

Politicians, ever mindful of next year's election, began making soothing noises about pushing the retirement age out a couple of years. Some governments borrowed. Others begged.

Talk around the world was soon of higher taxes, lower pensions, later retirement, and probably all three. The

> To depend on a retirement fund, either state or private, is probably a forlorn hope.

more pragmatic among us are already realizing that to depend on a retirement fund, either state or private, is probably a forlorn hope.

Young workers will only tolerate so much in taxation before leading a revolt at the ballot box, and private funds are stretched to the breaking point. Not to mention those facing huge losses after investing in questionable ventures, in a desperate attempt to stay ahead of the game and cover earlier losses.

> Many now face the prospect of living out their retirement in poverty.

As a result, many now face the prospect of living out their retirement in poverty, with that country club lifestyle a distant dream.

They can't rely on the state, they can't rely on the private funds, and they certainly can't rely on their children. The next generation is going to have to look after themselves and most haven't got the faintest idea how to go about it, because they've also bought into the retirement fallacy.

Of course there will be changes. We're already being conditioned to accept that workers born after 1960 will receive no benefit until they reach the age of sixty-seven.

That's pretty much a given. Pension plans are being rewritten to pay out more, the longer you put off the dreaded day. To our mind this is little more than a cynical ploy to sucker people into working longer in the hope they do the decent thing and "move on" before the day comes to pay out.

This brings us back to the earlier observation that the truly rich and successful don't retire. The Gateses and the Buffetts of this world have the financial wherewithal to stop earning, but they can't afford the intellectual or emotional stress. To retire would be to give up day-to-day control over what they've spent their whole lives building, because that's what retirement does to you. It takes away control and you end up living for the past rather than for the now and the

> The truly rich and successful have the financial wherewithal to stop earning, but they can't afford the intellectual or emotional stress.

future. Some people live their entire lives like that, but do you really want to be one of them?

There's even a notion that working on is somehow a manifestation of failure. "Oh, you haven't retired yet?" is always said in a pitying tone.

This is rather like the nine-to-five middle manager who asked his entrepreneur neighbor: "Are you busy?"

When the answer was a definite no, he instantly went into sympathy mode, completely failing to grasp that the self-employed and successful go-getter had structured his life around "working smarter not harder," being successful rather than busy.

Neil worked for a news organization that refused to run a drug investigation he'd spent six months researching, the story killed by gutless management because of pressure to protect the reputation of a friend of a high-powered politician.

It was a defining moment. Not only did Neil resign, he vowed he'd never again be dependent on a single employer or at the mercy or the whim of another individual. He set about establishing a diverse portfolio of clients and interests across a wide range of communication disciplines. He's now in charge of his own destiny and will be until the day he dies. And he has no intention of ever retiring, slowing down or working part-time. He just plans to get on with the rest of his life. And when people ask, "Are you busy?" he's learned to smile and reply, "Oh, I'm managing."

The question still remains—why have so many of us fallen for the retirement message? Why, despite all the evidence to the contrary, do we continue to march towards the cliff like the proverbial lemmings?

Why have so many of us fallen for the retirement message?

If you're still clinging fondly to the idea of retirement there's no need to feel bad about it—you've been conditioned to retire in the same way you've been conditioned to be polite and say "please" and "thank you." Just as these accepted courtesies come naturally to you, so retirement has become an accepted part of your life.

Well, excuse us, but we really don't find it acceptable to suggest to someone that they should metaphorically roll over and play dead. And what makes the whole situation even more farcical is that the very politicians in North America, Europe, and Australasia who are trying to keep the concept of retirement alive—even if it is by raising the age of qualification by a few years—are seeking to replace all the talent they are dumping on the scrap heap by encouraging great waves of immigration. And in the process of importing skills our older people already have, they are often stripping poorer countries of their most talented people, including the cornerstone of any civilized nation—its doctors, nurses, and teachers.

Instead they should consider the simple premise that the answer lies in scrapping retirement. Rather than telling people they are good for nothing more than a rocking chair,

> With every additional year comes greater wisdom, greater perception and far greater value.

they should spread the gospel that with every additional year comes greater wisdom, greater perception, and far greater value.

And that's the magic word: *value*, not price—we need to revert to a time when people didn't retire but were treasured for their knowledge and the extraordinary value they added to their community.

The average age of the population of most countries will soar in the next fifty years, including the countries from which many enlightened Western nations are currently poaching young talent.

With the first baby boomers entering their "golden years," there seems to be an endless stream of articles and books lauding how clever and how healthy and how rich they are. We're constantly reminded that the fifty-plus age group earns trillions and accounts for more than half of the world's discretionary spending power. And what's the message we send to all these incredibly valuable and important people? "Yes, we know you're healthy, wealthy, and incredibly wise. We accept, albeit grudgingly, that you control the vast majority of the planet's financial resources, but would you be so kind as to do everyone a terrific favor and call it a day?"

Not that all these decrepit souls who have turned sixty want to retire—quite a few are rather keen to keep going. When questioned, baby boomers—surely the most surveyed people on the face of the planet—reveal that four out of five would be keen on scrapping compulsory retirement, something that has now been done in some countries where there are agencies specializing in finding employment for the over-fifties.

Worldwide, consultants are making big money by showing companies how to motivate a highly age-diverse workforce, and attract and retain older workers "while meeting the development and career needs of younger workers."

On the face of it, this represents a total rejection of traditional retirement. It must be said, however, that most of the support for the idea of working through retirement is from those afraid of how they would survive in retirement without a pension.

That said, it's encouraging that in the United Kingdom recent surveys have shown that three in every four people thought working past retirement age was desirable. Again a word of caution: much of this discussion is couched in terms of lessening the pressure on pensions and taxation. Another survey found that, given a choice, Britons would like to retire as early as fifty-eight. All this confusion is taking place at a time when the British government is weighing up the pros and cons of forbidding companies from setting retirement ages and with talk of the state pension age being raised to seventy by 2030.

Encouraging as these signs are, they represent little more than a valiant attempt to put off the evil day.

It's important to note that none of this has anything to do with improving the quality of life of any of these "old" people; they're all just mechanisms to ease the pressure on the pension pot that is already beginning to implode. No one is being given a choice here—the people making the decisions are the politicians and the statisticians. Are you happy for the rest of your life to be left in their hands? We're not.

Instead of talking about not being able to afford to pay pensions, the discussion should be about how our society will crumble if we don't accept the valuable role to be played by people working to the very end of their days.

The power has shifted. There aren't enough young people coming through to run the shop. Right now you're in the driving seat. The trick is to firmly announce you have no intention of handing over the wheel, let alone jumping off while the vehicle is in motion.

> The retirement dream may be coming to an end, but there's no reason for it to be a nightmare.

What matters is that people who were once pigeon-holed as dispensable need to take control and write the rules. The retirement dream may be coming to an end, but there's no reason for it to be a nightmare.

Many companies are finding it increasingly difficult to recruit skilled staff, and that includes hi-tech industries. If we're getting through and you're thinking of scrapping your plans to retire, you can do so in the knowledge we're fast approaching a time when companies will be desperate to hang on to their older employees.

> We're fast approaching a time when companies will be desperate to hang on to their older employees.

All that matters now is your mindset—your attitude. It is crucially important that you don't think in terms of putting off retirement for a few years. The secret is to put it off forever.

> The secret is to put retirement off forever.

The time will of course come when you decide, for a host of personal reasons, to slow down—but at a time and a place of your choosing. For now you'll be in charge. You must be feeling better already.

Key points
to remember

☑ We can't rely on the state, private funds or our children to support us

☑ The fifty-plus age group controls more than half the world's discretionary spending

☑ The power has shifted. There aren't enough younger workers coming on behind and you're in the driving seat

4
Exploding the myth of retirement

Sorry to say this, but what follows is going to make depressing reading—a classic tale of man's inhumanity to man.

The myth of retirement is the result of generations of cruel manipulation of the human spirit. We're born with a strong natural urge to survive and yet we've been socially re-engineered and conditioned to believe that it's our predetermined lot to surrender on a given date.

> We've been socially re-engineered to believe that it's our predetermined lot to surrender on a given date.

It's patent nonsense of course, but hardly surprising given the nature of our current world order and the commercial imperatives that now drive us and most of the developed world. Money is supreme and we live in a world increasingly driven by price, not value.

We design appliances from motor cars to washing machines to anything you care to name, with built-in obsolescence. And should the appliance accidentally last longer than desired by the manufacturer and retailer, not to worry, they just design a different version. A "must have" new version—"must have" because the advertisements tell you so.

Clothes designers and manufacturers were probably the first to cotton on to this marketing truth. How to get the folk out there to buy a new coat when the one they already have is perfectly adequate? Simple. Make one that looks different, then parade it down a catwalk, draped over the shoulders of an impossibly thin young woman while the rich and famous gawk from the front row and the photographers go wild. Within days the general public will be banging on the front door screaming, "Must have! Must have!"

Sadly, it works. Year after year the fashion industry persuades hundreds of millions of people to throw out everything from underwear to shoes to suits to handbags and replace them with ones that look, well . . . different.

"You're wearing jeans with the knees artistically torn out. Darling! How terribly passé. You should really be wearing jeans classically frayed at the heel." All this from the very people who sold you torn knees the year before.

And while you may not have fallen for the distressed jeans nonsense, admit it, you are fashion-conscious. Or, to put it more correctly, you're conscious of not wanting to look different from everyone else.

Hence the new sneakers, the new shirt, the new washing machine, television and, when you come to think of it, the car *is* starting to look a bit dated. After all, what's the point of arriving, decked out from head to toe in all the latest fashion accessories, if the box on four wheels you drove up in sends all the wrong messages?

And that's what it's really all about. Sending messages. We've been conditioned to read signs and form opinions based on appearances—the way people speak and look, the clothes they wear, the cut of their hair, right down to the color of their skin and the car they drive. We judge them on where they live, the work they do and, most importantly, the title they hold.

We haven't actually met them, spoken with them. We haven't got a clue what they may or may not think about globalization, carbon taxes, the Middle East, or even the hidden messages in *Lost*. We don't know if they beat their children, have a criminal past, or attend Donny Osmond concerts.

But we do know what they wear and what they do and where they live. And, of course, what car they drive. Based on that we form our opinion of them in a nanosecond. Good, bad, or indifferent. Decision made.

Of course, we're acutely aware that people judge us by those very same trivial, irrelevant, and inconsequential criteria . . . so we buy into the brand business. And what a business. Branding has now become so important we've collectively been persuaded to become walking advertisements to help increase sales and, to add insult to injury, we pay a premium for the privilege. We're prepared to pay an inflated price to wear a brand that makes us instantly acceptable.

We even wear clothes with labels on the outside, just so we can demonstrate to the world at large that we can afford this or that particular brand. Doesn't seem to matter that the brand is Western and the country of origin Eastern, and cost next to nothing to make, thanks to the pittance paid to workers in some sweat shop.

What matters is how much it cost to *buy*. The brand tells everyone it was expensive. And somehow that makes you special. Well, we did warn you this would make depressing reading.

By some estimates, the brand-conscious among us pay up to ten times the price of an unbranded yet identical article, simply for the prestige that particular brand offers. Think about it. We're prepared to pay *ten times* more than we need to, just for the *label*.

The good news is that there comes a time when certain brands price themselves out of the market. Retirement is just such a brand.

To assist our own clients solve communication-related issues we've broken the battle for hearts and minds into five essential requirements:

- Perception
- Perception
- Perception
- Perception
- Perception

> **We live in a world where perception has become reality.**

We live in a world where perception has become reality.

The harsh reality is that retirement has been sold to us as a brand we should be happy to wear, cheerfully accepting that we can and should be discarded in much the same way as we toss out last year's shoes.

We shall return to the question of how our minds can be programmed and our behavior modified, but for now let's focus on how on earth we bought into this whole silly idea.

We've already seen that various players in the retirement industry are looking decidedly worried. To be fair, the experts are starting to ring warning bells about the financial sustainability of retirement. Questions are being raised

> Questions are being raised about whether we can afford to have people retiring early, or even at all.

about whether we can afford to have people retiring early, or even at all. With falling fertility rates, improved health and rising life expectancy, it's suddenly starting to dawn on the politicians that there simply isn't the money to support all these old codgers. The politicians who have caught a glimmer of the future are starting to talk down

> Social commentators the world over are seriously questioning the validity of a retirement policy.

workers' expectation of a state pension for them at the end of their working lives. Social commentators the world over are seriously questioning the validity of a retirement policy.

We've seen how there's a mind shift towards trying to persuade people to put off retiring until their late sixties, but we think that's missing the point—there's no real point in delaying retirement, we should be putting it off altogether. The trouble with politicians, and this applies to every variety, is that their political survival—which includes their own very generous pension plans—depends on the self-interest of the voter, hence their preoccupation with identifying powerful voting blocks and promising them anything they want. And what do people want more than anything else? Safety and security.

Safety and security typically boil down to the protection offered by quality education and health services combined with an efficient police force to guarantee our personal safety, not only on the streets but in our own homes.

Those are the essential basics, but the biggie—the one that transcends all else—is the security of knowing that the state will step in with a handout if you show the slightest sign of needing one. All modern societies are judged on how they care for the mentally ill and aged. Notice whom the elderly are so commonly bracketed with?

To satisfy the call for security following the Great Depression and two devastating world wars, politicians seized on the notion of the social welfare state and began selling it in one form or another to enthralled voters throughout the Western world. And it all began with a promise of instant utopia. Free education, free health care, free housing for the truly desperate, and financial support for the unemployed. And the absolute big prize was the promise of a pension to ensure everyone lived a happy and dignified retirement. Whether you saved for it or not, whether you deserved it or not—all you had to do was live long enough. Delivering on these pledges was dependent on sufficient taxes being raised, but the promise of such largesse came at a time when Europe and the United States were rebuilding after two crippling world wars which had also claimed the lives of millions of young men, creating a booming employment market.

> The absolute big prize was the promise of a pension to ensure everyone lived a happy and dignified retirement.

Filled with relief at having come through the Second World War unscathed, the survivors set about celebrating with a passion. The result, a massive upswing in the birth rate and the arrival of that phenomenon we now refer to as baby boomers. They in turn put huge pressure on the health and education services.

Surprise, surprise, there were now people putting out their hands to be paid from the public purse because they couldn't find work. Then, to compound matters, the ones who were working, were better educated, and smarter than ever before, began discovering even more ways to manufacture sought-after goods by employing machines rather than people.

And it didn't end there. Enter the good people of Asia with their own version of the industrial revolution that quickly accelerated the technology and microchip revolution that had begun in the United States. They began making cheap transistor radios, but soon stereo systems, televisions, computers, and cars with every conceivable extra, began emerging. At first they were shameless copies, but in short order the enterprising engineers of Japan, Taiwan, and Korea discovered they could add vast technological improvements, and then radical new products, while at the same time reducing costs.

In a technological blink, the West was confronted not only by a ballooning population but also by its industrial heartland coming under siege from the emerging export-driven economies of Asia. Never forget the sleeping economic giant, China, who is now also entering the fray.

As economic histories go, we're the first to concede that's about as simplistic as they come. Greater minds than

ours have produced worthy tomes
on the subject. The bottom line
is that once-dominant economies
are now pondering the millstone
of social welfare. How do we fund
the health care of a rapidly ageing
population? How do we continue

> Once-dominant economies are now pondering the millstone of social welfare.

to provide quality education? How do we support the
growing army of unemployed and unemployable?

The answer has been a discreet dismantling of the welfare
state. The word "free" being gradually replaced by the ever-
so-friendly sounding "subsidized" and "user pays."

Of course education is still "free," but there'll be a small
surcharge depending on the area you live in. The poorest
pay nothing, but no parent in their right mind wants
their child to go to a school in such an area. Everyone
else pays top-up fees, usually to attract the best teachers.
One of the great ironies of modern life is that the new
world economy requires skilled workers, yet is serviced by
a failing education system in just about any country you
care to name.

Health is still talked of as being "free," but with a
small additional fee depending on how much you earn.
Unfortunately, most public health services are so run down
that even a small surcharge does little to ease the pain. In
most developed countries around the world, the truly poor
tend to be particularly ignorant on health matters, while
everyone else digs deep to afford medical insurance.

The police force is still there of course, providing its services free of charge, but increasingly it is under-resourced; and in many countries we see the rich moving into gated communities with their own security guards, while everyone else joins neighborhood watch schemes and prays.

As well as this shortfall in basic services, social welfare programs, initially designed to give short-term relief to the deserving, have become a state insurance scheme to keep the unemployable from forming an angry mob at the gate of civilized society.

If all that sounds too insensitive, we could rewrite it with politically correct platitudes to make everyone feel better, or we could just accept the harsh reality and move on.

Which brings us to the retirement business, with "business" being the only word for it. Let's recap:

- We're conditioned to being put out to pasture to create job vacancies.

- The falling birth rate and failing education system mean there are now fewer new skilled workers.

- Smarter companies are moving to retain and even retrain their more mature employees. The ones over fifty.

But out there in the real world, the vast majority of people continue to suffer from that dreadful pre-programming: they will retire. Why? Because we've been conditioned to believe that's the way it should be, which simply isn't true. Human beings are born survivors—all our natural instincts and evolutionary programming tell us to keep going and live life to the full.

We're not encouraging some silly notion of living to be 120. We're all going to die—of course we are—but there's absolutely nothing in our past to suggest the slightest desire to surrender. Our very being revolves around a desire to live, and retiring has nothing to do with living. Remember the definition—*to remove from view; withdraw from society.*

> Our very being revolves around a desire to live, and retiring has nothing to do with living.

That's what society expects of us at a certain age. Well, given the failure of that same society to provide the comfort blanket of health, education, and security, why on earth would we even contemplate obeying that final instruction?

Right now we can hear you muttering away under your breath, "That's fine and dandy for you to say, but what can I do about it? How do I actually avoid retirement?"

We're faced with a slight dilemma here, as everyone is different and needs to create solutions to meet their individual needs, but we're assuming the notion of "not retiring" now has some appeal, either to retain your finances or sanity, and hopefully both.

The first cold hard fact you're going to have to come to terms with is that the solution is in your hands and your hands alone. No one is going to offer you the answer on a plate.

> The solution is in your hands and your hands alone. No one is going to offer you the answer on a plate.

So the first thing you have to do is reiterate that earlier pledge to banish the very word "retirement" from your vocabulary. It no longer exists as a serious option.

That's quite an achievement in itself, as a full third of all American men over the age of fifty-five no longer work, and that statistic is being repeated the world over. Not all of them have retired in the strictest sense, of course—many were laid off or lost their jobs and find themselves the victim of market forces that discriminate against anyone aged fifty or over.

It's sad, it's unfair, and there's nothing you can do about it. Nonsense! Of course you can do something about it. For a start, you can stop behaving like a victim. As of now you have to start thinking about your real life. What's been has gone—so no more remembering the good old days and moping about what could have been. Start thinking about the rest of your life. Now you're thinking!

More to the point, you're now acting like someone with a life ahead of you, rather than a life behind you. Notice what a difference that makes to the way you feel? A life ahead of you, not a life behind you. Instead of retirement, think about renewal, rejuvenation, and the whole new world that's opened up before you. Now that you've taken responsibility for yourself, you can decide what to do with the rest of your life.

Here we issue our standard warning: this is not some New Age message about finding your-self by hiking in the great outdoors or joining a choir or—heaven forbid—backpacking around the world. Do any of these by all means, but they're not the answer. The sole aim here is to continue onward and upward to a more enriching and rewarding life, with "life" the operative word. We were born to perpetual motion—stop and you die.

> The aim is a more enriching and rewarding life.

> We were born to perpetual motion—stop and you die.

For proof of that, visit a typical old folks' home where you'll find a dozen or so people—some still in their sixties—seated in armchairs, arranged in a semi-circle, blankets over their knees, watching television while they sip tea.

On second thought, don't do anything of the sort. During research for this book we visited just such a home and took with us one of our former clients, now in his eighties and still chairing a number of significant boards.

After a few minutes he excused himself, leaving us to our interviews with the residents. When we found him later in the garden, he explained, "I'm sorry, I had to leave, it was so depressing."

That's why all the current talk of *delaying* retirement for an extra few years is such a fallacy. It misses the point entirely; all that achieves is to assist poorly performing governments, and the managers of failing pension funds worried about how to make all the payments that are coming due. It is only delaying the inevitable when they have to admit the system is bankrupt. All of this will come as a huge shock to the deluded who fell for the story in the first place. Deluded souls who bought into the great myth of retirement, and they number in the tens of millions all over the world.

There are exceptions, of course.

Andrew and Sandra were sailing their forty-foot yacht deep in the South Pacific when Andrew suffered a mild stroke. Between them, they managed to find safe harbor and medical care. As it was, everything turned out fine, but it prompted them to re-evaluate their situation.

They were running a wholesale electrical business,

catering to trade and industrial customers, a business they'd started forty-five years earlier. Their first decision was to find something more manageable for Sandra, who was starting to have problems with her joints and was unable to cope with their three-storey home. They did the unthinkable. They moved into a lifestyle village, buying a three-bedroom, two-bath home with a double garage.

Note: they chose a lifestyle village, rather than a retirement village. They weren't giving up, and had no plans to retire. They continued to commute daily to their business, Sandra driving her bright red, low-slung Mitsubishi 3000GT VR-4, a neck-snappin', head-turnin', pavement-grabbin', road-shreddin', turbo-spinnin' machine.

Earlier they'd taken on a twenty-one-year-old assistant. He now owns 40 percent of the company, to give him a real incentive to keep growing the business while Andrew and Sandra are away traveling the world, with Andrew in demand as a respected international yachting judge. As it is, the last fifteen years have been the most successful for their business, ensuring they never get bored.

As for leisure, they've replaced the yacht with a forty-one-foot motor cruiser so they can take their children and grandchildren away for long weekends.

It never entered their heads to retire, although Andrew often jokes that they're saving for the moment. Did we mention their ages? Andrew is eighty while the girl racer is a traffic-stoppin' eighty-two.

You too can avoid the disappointment, misery, and the sheer waste of your potential by refusing point-blank to sign up to the misconception that is retirement. Now is the time to plan for what will be an active and rewarding rest of your life.

> Put all that background and experience to real effect by working smarter, not harder.

Not that we're suggesting for one moment that you set about working yourself into an early grave. Far from it. As you'll see, we're suggesting you put all that background and experience to real effect by working smarter, not harder.

Now that "retirement" no longer exists in your vocabulary, you can set about *living* the rest of your life.

Key points
to remember

✓ Retirement is a brand which has priced itself out of the market

✓ Social commentators worldwide are questioning the sustainability of retirement policies

✓ When you stop thinking about retirement, your focus is on the life ahead of you, not the life behind you

✓ We were born to perpetual motion—stop and you die!

5

The chickens are coming home to roost

Finally, the world is waking up to the reality that retirement is no longer sustainable. All around the world, most countries have set aside a pittance in retirement funds. Australia is better off than most, thanks to a compulsory superannuation scheme, with the United States not far behind. Even so, it's estimated that every household in the United States owes more than $500,000 for financial promises made to this generation. This brings the US Government's unfunded obligations to $57.8 trillion and pay-day starts in 2008.

No one seems to be taking this shortfall between expectation and reality seriously. Or, should we say, no government is taking this seriously. Oh, they're worried about it—after all, they're facing a looming financial burden and recognize their inability to deal with it.

This is a double-barrelled problem. Not only is there insufficient money to fund the looming retirement bulge, but treating the health problems of the growing army of old-age pensioners is going to be nearly impossible. Most health systems are already creaking at the seams and on the verge of terminal collapse. From Britain to New Zealand we see the farce of sick people, many in considerable pain, being shifted from one waiting list to another in a statistical charade aimed at persuading the populace at large that the health system is working.

Relying on a private medical scheme when you are older isn't the answer either. Each year medical premiums will increase until they become financially unsustainable. Also, your private health scheme may not cover the more serious age-related ailments.

It's no wonder then that the best solution is first and foremost to not retire and to take a pro-active approach to health care—stay as fit and healthy as you can, for as long as you can, and never, ever, give up. No health system is a safety net; at best they provide a perception of security, which may or may not be there when you need it.

> Stay as fit and healthy as you can, for as long as you can, and never, ever, give up.

Health aside, most of us don't have a clue as to what we might realistically expect to receive in our "retirement" years, a combination of what the government might fork out and what we might have saved. Governments and politicians see everything in financial terms and we have been conditioned to do likewise. They deal in problems and generally survive by offering solutions to problems at the bottom of the cliff. Why? Because that's where the votes are.

> Governments deal in problems and generally survive by offering solutions to problems at the bottom of the cliff.

Sadly, wherever you are in the world, the promise of everlasting health care and support in retirement is a hollow promise. The chickens are well and truly coming home to roost, with no Western country having sufficient funds to fulfill the promises they have made to their citizens regarding health and retirement.

To be perfectly blunt about this, if you've read this far and you still think it's a good idea to hand over the responsibility for the rest of your life to a politician, any politician, you're probably beyond help.

Please, wean yourself off the rhetoric and see it for what it is. Rhetoric. Has the health sector in recent years improved because of government intervention? Will your prospects in retirement improve? But, not to worry, they are waiting for you at the bottom of the cliff. Terrific. The answer of course is not to take that great leap of faith.

Keep your feet planted firmly on the ground and take back control of your life.

- You are never going to retire.

- You are going to stay active and productive.

- You are going to do all the things you once planned to do when you retired.

Refuse to be part of a manufactured crisis, rather like the

> Refuse to be part of a manufactured crisis.

hoopla around the Y2K crisis. Remember that one? As clocks ticked past midnight into the new millennium of 2000, it was predicted that computers the world over would crash. The lights would go out, financial markets would be thrown into crisis, and nuclear missiles launched. It proved to be a crisis with no foundation. Computer software is designed on two digits, one and zero—no one had designed a software program with instructions to collapse on being confronted by two zeros. Yet the world went into a blind panic, spending trillions of dollars to prevent a purely imaginary crisis. And when the clocks ticked past midnight, and the world kept quietly spinning, there was hardly a moment of embarrassed silence. Ah, well, better safe than sorry.

Retirement is another Y2K—with bells on. Retirement is presented as a looming mountain of seemingly insoluble problems and, as they say, seeing is believing. But is there really a "retirement mountain"? Is the situation inevitable and insoluble? What if we're actually trapped in a hall of mirrors? How do you find your way out of a mirror maze and back to reality? The answer is simple—don't look at the mirrors, look down at your feet and follow the most well-worn path. In the same way, to get out of the retirement maze follow your own feet along the path that has served you best throughout your life. Take your eyes off the mirrors and look at your feet. Consider what's worked before. Follow your own path and practice what you've preached all your life to this point. Why even consider changing now?

You are highly likely to have tried to stay healthy and alive, and worked for pleasure and reward in equal quantities. If you don't live like that, then start doing so immediately and continue doing so forever.

It really is that simple. If you refuse to retire, how can you become part of the retirement problem? Perhaps it would be good to have it as a mantra: "I'm not retiring, I'm not part of the problem, I'm going to get on with my life."

> If you refuse to retire, how can you become part of the retirement problem?
>
>

Of course the merchants of doom will tell you it can't be done. You could listen to them and invest in their get-rich-quick schemes as they tell you that not retiring is too silly for words. It can't be done. You have to retire, everyone does.

Chris and Judy are a classic example of how people get caught up in this process. They both had careers but when they decided to have a family Judy stayed home to become a full-time mother. Soon there were four children and, before they knew it, they were caught with the escalating costs of education and health care and, of course, saving for their retirement.

What a dilemma. How could they meet all these costs on a single income? Should Judy go back to work? How much was enough? How much could they save on a single income? Could they save anything?

That's when they took our advice and removed the "R" word from their vocabulary, along with the whole dilemma of how to avoid ending up at the bottom of the cliff. They decided not to jump. Instead Chris and Judy have reorganized their affairs for continued sustainability. They're actively seeking occupations that will engage and sustain them long-term and they're focused on developing working lives with ongoing prospects. They're most certainly not squandering their savings, nor are they thinking in terms of retirement investments.

Now that Chris and Judy are in the marathon, and not the sprint, life has become much easier. They can now pace themselves. No more competing with the Joneses for ever-smarter toys. They're relaxed and will now replace their cars when they need to, not every few years as had been the case. Their home has now become a real sanctuary—a philosophical choice, not a financial one. They're no longer looking at a bigger and brighter house in an even wealthier suburb, they're simply happy to pay off the one they have and settle in for the long haul. Time that would have been spent looking at new houses is now spent getting to know their neighbors and becoming a vital part of their community. And yes, you've guessed it, their lives are more enriched, and they no longer fear the future as they both plan ongoing careers.

We can't give you the happy ending to this story, as both Chris and Judy have yet to determine precisely how their lives will pan out. Should they set up a joint business? Should they diversify their talents? Should they embark on an entirely new venture?

Whatever the decision, it will work for them as they've grasped the essential requirement; they have no intention of retiring. They have their lives back, and they're getting on with enjoying the rest of their lives. They came to an intersection and, faced with the choice of going left or right, they decided to listen to their intuition.

If you have any doubt, then recognize that doubt for what it is: a warning of obstacles ahead. Problems your subconscious mind has seen and is trying to warn you about. At this point, it's not about "proceed with caution," it's more a case of "proceed at your peril."

The simple, direct route always tends to be best. There can be no better example of this than the Gordian knot. In 333 BCE the great warrior Alexander the Great was leading his armies on his conquest of Asia. On arriving at the gates of the city of Gordium in Phrygia, he was welcomed by the local citizenry who led him to a chariot, once owned by a founder of the ancient city. The chariot was tied to a pole with an intricate and complex Turkish knot that left no ends exposed. Over time this knot consisting of hundreds of tightly interwoven threads of bark had hardened into an impenetrable mass. Legend had it that whoever undid the Gordian Knot would rule all of Asia.

Alexander stared long and hard at the puzzling knot, then drew his sword and with one swift stroke cut the formidable knot in two. Decisive action from a man who did indeed go on to conquer and unite all of Asia.

The moral of this story? Don't get too tied up in a problem. Be bold!

> Beneath all complexity lies simplicity.

Beneath all complexity lies simplicity, and the answer to the seemingly complex problem of retirement is simply *not to retire*. Think of it as a knotty problem that can be solved with decisive action. And once you're off the retirement treadmill, you'll wonder why you ever got on it in the first place. You'll watch governments and individuals still struggling with this huge knot, of Gordian dimensions, and smile wryly to yourself.

The message is getting through, and others are taking direct action. There are now supermarkets in Britain that actively employ and encourage an older workforce. They're proving to be more popular and more profitable than supermarkets that follow the traditional trend of employing younger people. It seems people over fifty are more cheerful, more polite, take fewer days off and pilfer less—which all adds up to a better shopping experience and improved profits.

> People over fifty are more cheerful, more polite, take fewer days off and pilfer less.

The experiment started way back in 1989 when B&Q, the biggest chain of do-it-yourself stores in Britain, decided to try to overcome their high staff turnover rate. They opened a store in the town of Macclesfield and staffed it exclusively with people over the age of fifty. The results were astounding. Over a six-month period that operation returned profits 18 percent above the national average for stores in the group; staff turnover was six times lower; and absenteeism was down a whopping 39 percent. And to top it all, their shoppers reported improved perception of customer service.

This example was swiftly picked up on by the supermarket chain Sainsbury's, with its 170,000 employees. They deliberately targeted older workers, and, such was the success, they extended contributions to their pension scheme up to the age of seventy-five.

Another company to travel this path is Kappa Packaging, the third largest packaging company in Europe with six United Kingdom plants. A third of their workforce is over fifty, with 75 percent over forty years old and a staggering average length of employment of fifteen years. They've publicly proclaimed, "Our continuing profitability and success is testament to the commitment, loyalty, and productivity of our older workers."

What started as an experiment has been so successful that more and more major employers are latching onto the idea, with the Age Positive Council in the United Kingdom now listing more than eighty companies as champions of the cause.

But what about the young people? What about them? There's no monopoly on being cheerful, polite, having fewer days off, and pilfering less. Younger people can try a bit harder. They can be just as competitive as they like. Since when were youth on some sort of pedestal that gave them a built-in advantage over their elders?

Don't get us wrong here. We're not for one moment saying that occupations should be age-selective. Quite the reverse. We're saying age is irrelevant to getting the work done; you can be competitive at any age. All it may take is a determination to turn up on time and not steal from your employer. That doesn't sound too difficult, does it?

> Age is irrelevant to getting the work done; you can be competitive at any age.

You really do have choices. You can sit around, do nothing, and live in hope that someone will take care of you at the bottom of the cliff. Or you can take responsibility for your own life, take it back under your control, and get on with living a useful and fulfilling life with your relationships and health all in good balance.

And as for tomorrow, ponder these wise words: "Look after today and tomorrow will take care of itself."

Key points
to remember

✓ Do what you need to stay fit and healthy

✓ Work for pleasure and reward in equal measure—continue doing this forever

✓ Refuse to become part of the problem and stay at the top of the cliff

6

Now live in a little box

One of the most unsettling aspects of retirement is how society presumes we will need less as we get older. Really?

Why are any of us so silly as to go along with this nonsense? The answer is we've been emotionally hijacked, our thought processes captured and conditioned to believe that winding down is

> Society presumes we will need less as we get older. Really?

natural and good for you, the best thing you can do. Best for whom, though, is the question. Best for ourselves or for the system that presumes to know best?

This is the insidious retirement virus at work. The good news is you have a magnificent in-built anti-virus program—your intuition. All you need to do is give your intuition free rein and it will quickly conclude that retirement has no place in your life.

Now—and this is the crucial moment—you must listen to yourself, to your intuition, and act on it. No one

> Listen to yourself, to your intuition, and act on it.

understood this better than the psychologist Daniel Goleman, one of the great minds of our time. He concluded, and scientifically demonstrated, that the emotional or intuitive brain is quite capable of hijacking the rest of the brain and, subsequently, our thinking and actions—it's not only capable and adept at this, but it's programmed to do just that.

This is quite extraordinary, as our brain is driven by a central force, buried deep in its core, and known affectionately as the "lizard level" or reptilian brain. This is our genetic inheritance, our blueprint for survival—the essence of our existence that dictates our very being, in effect a "control center" active from the moment of conception.

Nothing, absolutely nothing, in this "control center" is telling you to retire. Quite the reverse, it is telling you to live. Survive. At any cost.

Yet, somehow, our reptilian brain has been re-programmed. The "lizard level" in us has been infected with the great misconception of retirement. Most people we know in this predicament seem to adopt the "growth for growth's sake" principle, and then enough can never be enough. Perhaps it's worth noting here that growth for the sake of growth is also the principal function of the cancer cell.

Now, without wishing to get all political and Karl Marx about this, we appear to have been predestined to serve a system that is woefully ill-prepared to cope. There is no promised land. It's all an illusion. And what can you do about it? Well, one thing is blatantly obvious: waiting for the government, any government, to intervene is a complete waste of time. There are no votes in prevention. There are no votes in fixing a problem before people know it exists. The votes are at the bottom of the cliff, where troubled and grateful souls reward politicians at the voting booth.

> Waiting for the government, any government, to intervene is a complete waste of time.
>
>

Fear is the shadow of safety; they go hand in hand. And, because fear is more direct and compelling, saying you can do something about it is a great vote winner.

Just look at our jails, they're full to overflowing, and what do the politicians promise? You're right, more jails. There are no votes to be had in talking about the comparative costs of prevention versus building more jails. So, more jails it is. This despite mounting evidence they're not the answer.

Britain's most senior judge, Lord Phillips, the Lord Chief Justice, has maintained that in his country's seriously overcrowded penal system "Prison is not the place for minor criminals. Punishment is important but it does not tackle the underlying cause of the offending." We wish his Lordship well in getting that message through to the vote-hungry politicians. This is the very same breed of politicians who want to lock us all up in retirement homes.

In both instances, they know the system has failed, they know it is bankrupt, but they keep on selling it as a somehow worthwhile and desirable idea. And we follow, like lambs to the slaughter.

In abattoirs, where the lambs are slaughtered, they make use of a well-trained Judas sheep. The frightened animals know there is danger ahead, they sense the impending doom, but blindly follow the Judas sheep into the race that leads to the slaughter yards. Needless to say, the Judas sheep is plucked to safety in the nick of time.

To follow the retirement theme, without thinking it through, is akin to following your own Judas sheep. Now, before you accuse us of being unduly harsh and judgmental here, think for a moment. What's the difference between a flock of sheep thinking they'll be OK so long as they stick together and follow their leader, and humans who pray silently before ambling into the holding pen of retirement?

The ultimate act of blind acceptance must be to stand upright, have the last farewell party and then march obediently into the oblivion of retirement. Oh yes, the farewell party, where your colleagues shuffle from foot to foot as all those embarrassing speeches are made. If you want to know what they'll be saying at your funeral, pop along to your retirement party. All those vibrant people, some perhaps just a year or so younger than you, hardly able to contain their impatience as they wait for you to totter off into the night clutching your farewell present, so they can get on and have a real party after the poor old sod has gone.

> If you want to know what they'll be saying at your funeral, pop along to your retirement party.
>
>

The alternative is to get a life, take control of your own destiny and be responsible. It can be done—take our dear friend Nancy.

Nancy is forever being sent questionnaires with a box to check, marked with that dreadful word "retired." This has her stumped, as she wonders whether this refers to retired from paid work, unpaid work, or even life itself. We should explain that Nancy is now eighty, and, while she could quite easily continue charging for her renowned skill as a mediator and arbitrator, she prefers to do pro bono work.

She also delivers meals-on-wheels to those less fortunate and gives her time as a "greeter" at one of

New York's busiest new visitor centers. In her spare time, she is training to be a public speaker for the Alzheimer's Association by way of giving something back to an organization that helped so much when one of her family was stricken by the illness. You can see her problem: is she retired?

Nancy certainly doesn't feel retired. She has a reason to get up every morning and can't wait for her new day to start—a day full of new challenges, new problems and, most importantly of all, a chance to meet new people and be exposed to new ideas, cultures, and values. A day to challenge and enthrall her. As a result, Nancy is experiencing a continual growing process, a learning process she never tires of, and indeed, looks forward to.

There has been a downside. Along the way, Nancy began to notice ever-so-subtle changes in some of her long-time friends. More to the point, she noticed they weren't changing. They seemed to have given up on the growing process, and they'd been left behind. It was never intentional; Nancy just woke up one morning and wondered what had happened to them. She'd moved on with her life while they were stuck in "retire" mode. Nancy has since gathered new friends and, while she does regret the loss of the old ones, she realizes they aren't actually lost, they're just stuck in a time and place she no longer wishes to be.

Nancy recognizes this as a necessary loss because if she hadn't moved on, she'd be stuck there too. Trapped in the past with no future—a future that includes an active working schedule, eating well, two-weekly visits to the gym and studiously ignoring any temptation to check the little "retired" box.

Nancy is not alone.

John was in his late fifties when he fell off a roof and broke half the bones in his body. Frowning doctors told John he'd spend the rest of his life in a wheelchair; he should accept his lot and take early retirement.

John wasn't having any of that. He spent every morning at his local swimming pool, forcing his aching body through a rigorous exercise regime. Every afternoon found him at the gym, pumping iron to strengthen his back, his stomach, and his weakened legs. It took him eight long months to prove the doctors wrong—and then he mortgaged his home to set up a takeout restaurant. Not for him a life of being housebound, bedridden, and dependent on the state.

In case you're wondering, John was a factory worker with no great skills—what he did have was a huge desire to create a better life for himself and his family, all driven and made possible by an enthusiasm for independence. Business boomed and soon there was a second shop and a celebratory world cruise for John and his wife, who continue to oversee their ever-expanding business as John approaches his seventieth birthday with no intention of slowing down.

They still have that wheelchair in their basement. They keep it as a reminder of what could have been. It serves as an inspiration to us all.

Don't retire. Stay away from those Judas sheep and the holding pens.

Our friends Phil and Denise had a narrow escape.
They're both intelligent people in their mid-sixties.
Both were in the process of planning an imminent,
self-inflicted retirement when they made the mistake
of inviting us out for lunch.

The food was delicious, but we soon lost our
appetite and sat there open-mouthed as these two
spelled out their plans. They said their remaining
useful lifespan was about five years. Their very
words—five years! We couldn't believe what we
were hearing. "Five years," we kept repeating in a
state of shock. Five years, they assured us. They'd
even purchased their last little car to see themselves
out and were planning to spend those last five years
in a small new home.

To say we were aghast would be an understatement. We were staring at what we knew would
become a self-fulfilling prophecy.

Lunch was longer than we anticipated, but by
the time we left, the harebrained idea of death by a
thousand cuts over five years was out the window,
as were the retirement plans, along with those silly
ideas about packing up and moving somewhere
smaller.

Instead they were planning an extended holiday and excitedly working out how to work less and perhaps earn even more. As for selling their family home, that was most definitely off the agenda. Now they were planning to stay where the action was— where their community was.

> By reorganizing your work life, you can continue to have a life.

One of the big insights for Phil and Denise was to recognize that by reorganizing their work life they could continue to have a life. No more talk of being dependent on an income from their fixed capital or worrying about whether they might outlive their resources.

> It's *your* freedom and *your* independence; *your* decision and *your* decision alone.

Imagine living like that! But people do. Please don't let it be you. Remember, no matter what other people may advise, it's *your* freedom and *your* independence they're talking about. It's *your* decision and *your* decision alone.

The secret behind the happy ending to Phil and Denise's story is simple enough. It revolves around a simple change of attitude. From being slaves to the whims of others, they took back charge of their own lives. And who gave them permission to change? They did, of course.

That's the crux of beating the curse of retirement. Get back in charge of your own life, your own existence. Ask why you're even thinking of retiring. Why do you have to retire when you reach sixty or sixty-five?

> Get back in charge of your own life, your own existence. Ask why you're even thinking of retiring.

> — Is it because you have to?

> — Because someone says you have to?

> — Because it's the thing to do?

None of the above are answers—they're poor excuses.

You may have to reorganize your life, change what you do or how you do it, but there is no earthly reason why you should have to retire.

You must grasp, as Phil and Denise did, that the only person who should have the power to predetermine what happens in your life is you. That's all it took for them; all they needed was to reconnect with their own intuitive base, and from that moment on they were back in charge of their lives. Now they were planning what was best for *them*, not someone else.

Sound selfish? You bet. That's the whole purpose of switching

> Reconnect with your intuitive base, and from that moment on you'll be back in charge of your life.

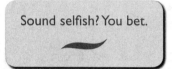

Sound selfish? You bet.

on your intuition. It works, just like magic, every time, and it's free. Try it for yourself.

Always remember: treat any doubts you may harbor as a positive warning. You may have noticed that whenever change is in the wind you slow down. That's what doubt does—it triggers the slowing mechanism to give you time to think the situation through and decide on the best response for you.

> If you still feel uncomfortable, another useful tip is to do nothing. This enables you to buy time while you work out what's really best for you.

If you still feel uncomfortable, another useful tip is to do nothing. Not because you don't know what to do, but because actively doing nothing can often be an excellent option. This enables you to buy time while you work out what's really best for you. For example, someone says you should retire and move into Happy Oaks Rest Home, but you just don't feel right about it. Well, do nothing. Don't argue the merits or demerits, simply do nothing and carry on as if it's not even an issue. Why put a time frame on yourself? Happy Oaks Rest Home can wait—they may need you, but do you need them? Given time to think, we venture to suggest the answer will be "Certainly not."

Take the case of Brent.

Brent was an admired headmaster in the United States who had parents lining up to enroll their children in his school. Retirement loomed and the community was busy organizing a farewell party, with former students flying in to pay homage and testify to the difference Brent had made to their now successful lives. They all attributed their success to this inspirational teacher. He'd reached that certain age and retirement was his due. To an outsider, his prospects looked terrific. What more could you want than to retire into a community where you are loved and respected?

What Brent wanted was to maintain his active life. He didn't want to see it shrivel into some retirement home. So what did he do? He packed up his courage and moved to the bottom end of the globe, and set up a school in the Southern Hemisphere where students now come from all over the world to "find themselves" in an environment geared to self-discovery rather than purely academic pursuits. A summer school for the Northern Hemisphere.

Could Brent have retired? Easily. Will he ever retire? Never. Why should he? He's found a new and rewarding niche and his new life is just beginning.

Did he accept the predetermined sentence to end his career? Not on your life, and certainly not on his. If he had, a large number of young people would have missed out on the life-enriching experiences he's been able to provide them, and the world at large would be all the poorer.

Last we heard from Brent, he was catching up on his e-mails before joining students happily kayaking about the coast. Just think: his alternative was to sit in a big soft chair somewhere and wait.

He had the answer. Make your own decisions. And let's have no more of this retirement virus malarkey.

Key points to remember

✓ Growth for growth's sake is the principal function of a cancer cell

✓ When in doubt, wait—listen to your intuition

✓ Give yourself permission to take charge of the rest of your life

✓ Reorganize your life, change what you do or how you do it, but don't stop doing it!

7

The retirement virus malarkey

Earlier we touched on rational and intuitive thought, the crucial roles they play in our decision-making process, and how they've come to influence our thinking towards retirement. Now's the time to explore this further. For ease of explanation and simplicity, imagine your brain is divided into two main compartments, with the intuitive to the right and the rational to the left.

The right or intuitive brain is programmed for your personal survival; "Live and do anything you need to do to be safe and survive." It's an intuitive sounding-board for what's right and wrong *for you*. As we've already explained, it's also sometimes referred to as the "lizard level" of the brain, or your reptilian brain, because it was there right at the beginning of human evolution. This is where your own personal anti-virus program lives.

Your left brain deals in rational matters, the black and white, and it's highly susceptible to outside programming. It's through this part of your brain that you're conditioned to accept the essential structures in our society. Like retirement planning. By now, the retirement virus has been deeply embedded and cleverly disguised as essential, not only to our own survival but to that of our society. In effect, we've all been preconditioned to believe retirement is a rational and legitimate expectation.

The intuitive part of our brain controls our organic functions and emotions and it's from here we derive our EQ (emotional quotient), whereas our IQ (intellectual quotient) comes from the processing part, our rational brain. This brings us to the argument of nature (right brain) versus nurture (left brain), or put another way, EQ versus IQ.

Step back a little, to 2005 when a story made headlines around the world: "Crisis Deepens as Apology Plea Rebuffed." Relations between China and Japan were at their lowest point in decades with reports of the powerful neighbors on a war footing. Both sides were said to be "talking past each other."

International response saw $178 billion wiped off the stock market. Why? What had brought these two super-powers to the brink of war? Were major untapped oil reserves at stake? Was a strategic land-grab involved? A spy scandal perhaps? On the surface, it was nothing so significant. The world was on the edge of its seat because of the emotions triggered by a controversial visit to a cemetery.

Japan's then Prime Minister, Junichiro Koizumi, had paid his respects at the Yasukuni Shrine where Japan's war dead are buried, and in the process created a major diplomatic incident with China, where bitter memories linger of the Second World War. From the Chinese perspective, Japanese aggression caused tens of millions of deaths and over $1 trillion of financial losses in the Asia-Pacific region.

While the Germans built a monument in memory of massacred Jews, the Japanese hung their war criminals and then buried them in sacred ground, along with 2.5 million military war dead, at the shrine visited by the Prime Minister.

Two countries were seriously at odds over what the Chinese ambassador described as "hurt feelings," all because the Japanese weren't paying attention to what the Chinese were saying about what was, to them, a highly emotive and painful issue. From the Chinese perspective, the Prime Minister's visit gave official recognition to, and even worse seemed to honor, Japanese war criminals responsible for the deaths of countless Chinese in what were terrible and unforgivable crimes.

The Chinese were outraged because of what the right-hand side of the brain was telling them—not about what might be technically and legally correct but the incredibly powerful emotions of fairness and justice. Seen in this light, the Prime Minister's visit was grossly unjust. How could he be so insensitive? How could he publicly honor murderers?

After all, public honor and murderers make for strange bedfellows when viewed from a victim's perspective.

When people discuss their greatest fears and sorrows, they use entirely different thought processes and language. Fundamental changes in attitude occur, based on inner feelings, without the person concerned even recognizing what has happened.

So why do we need emotional intelligence? There's now clear scientific evidence of a shortcut to the "lizard level" of the brain. This can trigger an emotional response before the rest of the brain fully understands, or even processes, what is happening.

> An emotional response can be triggered before the rest of the brain fully understands, or even processes, what is happening.

It's also worth noting that intuition, or our emotional driver, is in the head, not the heart. This is where confusion arises, through a common misnomer: what most people call "emotional intelligence" is actually, and more correctly, "intuitive intelligence," a combination of your emotions and your reasoning.

Albert Einstein, who discovered the theory of relativity, wrote: "The intuitive mind is a sacred 'gift,' and the rational mind a faithful 'servant,' but we live in an age that has forgotten the gift and worships the servant." Even in 1905, as a brilliant though unrecognized scientist, he was able to define the clear difference between an instinctive or intuitive approach and a rational one, and then give his view of their respective use and value.

We need to grasp that when faced with a challenge the brain instantaneously makes an overall analysis, then makes a decision based on emotion or intuition and finally rationalizes or justifies that decision. Looking at it this way, we can conclude that emotion drives all decision-making.

Intuition is both genetic and experience-based, instantly evaluating all the input from sight, sound, touch, smell, and taste — this is why the right brain processes in pictures, and the left brain deals in words. We wouldn't survive without our intuition, because the left brain could never think, act, and finally get us to respond fast enough in words. To put it another way, for the benefit of computer buffs, the brain is capable of absorbing something in the region of 40 billion hits a second, and we can't put the words together quickly enough when the pressure is on to act fast. Think about times when something has happened and you've had to react instantaneously — instinctively — "without thinking" we often say. Well, your brain was processing, just not in words, but in emotion-driven actions.

A global Internet provider had thirty top lawyers spend a month reviewing the due diligence process for the takeover of a country's monopoly telephone provider. Their instructions were to read every document and red-flag the critical ones—those that had the "E" factor. None of the lawyers knew what the "E" factor was, so the American CEO of the bidding company flew from New York to enlighten them.

As he explained it, the "E" factor is the number of times the letter "e" appears any time one of the lawyers says "Jeeeeesus" when looking at any of the documents. The light dawned. He wasn't buying their legal knowledge, he was buying thirty years' experience and intuition from each and every one of them.

Again, and especially for the lawyers out there, nothing demonstrates this better than the jury system in a murder trial. Twelve people are selected, and while they need to be able to absorb and analyse facts, the crucial decisions will be based on their intuition—their ability to relate to that part of the brain where guilt sits and, by drawing on their own experiences, second-guess the accused person's "intent." Intent is what makes the difference between acquittal, manslaughter, and murder. Given the same set of facts, it is the "intent" of the person that defines the outcome.

So how and why does this happen?

Because all of our initial "intuitive" decisions are about safety, the left brain defaults to the right brain to ensure that any decision we make is going to be a safe one. This also applies to organizations and institutions, where the prime concern is for the safety of the institution. They develop "rules" which replace the right-brain function.

That's why most institutions and organizations are often driven by fear, almost always an irrational fear, for their own safety.

Why is this important ?

The next time you hear any organization — be it religious, commercial or political — proclaiming why they need you to do something, remember that the reason they expect you to do anything is in fact, often shorthand, for what is in their interest. You are asked regularly to sacrifice your own interests for those of the institution. The greater good!

Retirement is a classic example. The *reasons* given as to why you should retire include:

— You've reached retirement age.

— We need younger workers.

— Technology has moved on and you haven't.

— We can replace you with a machine.

All of these are rational reasons as to why you should give up working, and the list goes on and on. But note that none of them has anything to do with you as a person, a human being whose whole survival mechanism is screaming, "No! Don't give up!"

You *think* you must be wrong because everyone is telling you so. You assume, because everyone seems to agree, that they must be right. Listen to yourself. Listen to your own survival mechanism, your own intuition. No one knows

> You always have options, including changing your occupation.

what's better for you than your own good self. Remember, you always have options, including changing your occupation.

There's a rather ironic twist in this whole process. The word "retiring," with all its depressing right-brain connotations, is followed in Webster's dictionary by the word "retool," meaning to re-equip with new tools. Out with the old and in with the new. Yet the concept of retirement presumes people can't retool, while in reality it's what we do every day of the week as we confront a multiplicity of challenges.

This presumes that while a machine can be retooled, a human is incapable of change. Nonsense, the human brain can handle those 40 billion bits of information in a second; it's made for change. Be involved. Retool your mind. Don't get off life's train at some quiet siding—and if you already have, think seriously about getting back on.

Athletes are a perfect example. In competitive sports they spend five years as a Junior, between the ages of fourteen and nineteen, then fifteen years as an Elite Athlete, usually between the ages of twenty to thirty-five, then as many years as they care to keep going with the proud description of Master Athlete.

People are constantly amazed by the times and performances turned in by Masters of all ages, even those in their eighties. And even though athletes turn in their peak performances around the age of twenty-six, no one expects them to quit soon after their twenty-seventh birthday.

Quite the contrary, many older athletes are stars in their own right, with the news media happily following their exploits. The Masters relish the continuing challenges and regularly make changes to ensure they can carry on competing. They get to think smart, rather like the hare and the tortoise.

Remember Aesop's wise old fable? The speedy hare bragged endlessly about how fast he could run. This proved more than the tortoise could bear, and he finally challenged the surprised braggart to a race. The hare took off at a predictably fast pace before stopping to mock his opponent and even settle down to have a little rest. The slow but dependable tortoise strolled on by the sleeping hare and kept on plodding away until he came to the finish line. The startled hare awoke to find he'd been slowly yet soundly beaten. There are many morals to this popular tale, the favorite being—slow and steady wins the race.

> **Slow and steady wins the race.**
>
> ~

Of course, the hare could just as easily have run flat-out and won by a country mile. But, the tortoise showed it could get to the finish-line by adopting a sensible pace. The right attitude.

The tortoise wasn't retiring from life's race. And neither should you.

Key points
to remember

✓ Don't ignore your intuitive
   intelligence—value it

✓ Your intuitive mind is a gift; your
   rational mind a faithful servant

✓ The combination of your experience
   and intuition, gained over a lifetime,
   has value

✓ Don't stop—change and pace
   yourself

8

Take control of your destiny

We're naturally programmed to survive, not retire—and even if you have retired, it's possible to get your life back, take control of your own destiny and enjoy yourself.

Retirement is *not* our destiny, and we all have it within ourselves to control our own future. All we need to do is to find something to aim for and then set about making the dream a reality. Put very simply: all you have to do is apply a timetable to your wish list—that really is all it takes.

> We all have it within ourselves to control our own future.

Significantly, you must put aside all thought of surrender, and determine that you are not going to toe the conventional line when it comes to retirement. You came into this world naked and helpless, without a thought in your head other than to survive. And if you're here reading this book, that's what you've spent your entire life doing successfully, from playground to classroom to sports field

Survival is everything.

to workplace and even in your personal relationships. Survival is everything, and as you progressed through life you became all the more skilled and practiced in this very natural human ability.

So why on earth would you buy into the bizarre notion that all that effort was in preparation for the day when you would walk away from your productive life and stop dead in your tracks? It just doesn't make sense, and flies in the face of what we were put on this earth to do—survive and keep on fighting to survive.

Of course, you *are* going to die one day—we all are—but heaven forbid you go before your allocated time.

Paul is a very good friend and an even better doctor, further living proof that our retirement message works.

Several years ago he was clearly down in the dumps. His shoulders had slumped while his eyes had a defeated, dull glaze as he stared into the middle distance. His skin had the pallid, lifeless look of ancient parchment. Simply put, life was draining out of him. Our friend Paul looked in dire need of a doctor himself.

He finally admitted that his life wasn't as great as it looked. This once-vibrant, fifty-something young man was talking of retiring. He was about to turn his back on a flourishing consulting practice and join a third of the family doctors who were on the verge of retirement. There were ominous warning signs; the country was facing a critical shortage of doctors. And of the doctors planning to call it quits, more than half were aged between thirty-one and fifty—in the prime of their lives.

They couldn't take the long hours any more, complaining of sixty-hour weeks, whereas those not planning to retire were looking for the safety of employment with the government, as hospital doctors. The idea of having their own practice was no longer attractive, and Paul had bought into this. Our friend was about to walk away from his entire life's work.

So we talked. We talked of how unnatural retirement is; more of a nightmare than a dream ending. We made him question why he wanted to stop—instead of retiring, why wasn't he expanding his business?

That stopped him in his tracks. If all the other people his age were thinking of retiring, this left a great hole in the market. He could bring in more young doctors, hire a practice manager to do the dreaded paperwork and give him more time to himself. He could have his well-earned rest **and** work at a more leisurely pace.

We reminded him of his success, of the zeal he once had for his job, and asked where it had gone. We asked him, as a medical man, what deficit there might be in his DNA that he would wish to fly in the face of mankind's inherent desire to survive and instead give up the ghost?

When we could see we had his attention, we asked him our favorite question: "How many rich and successful people do you know who have retired and do nothing?"

That pretty much clinched it. He began preaching our message back to us. He didn't have a use-by date—he was just getting started! He knew the facts. His generation was fitter and healthier than any before. What was he thinking of? He wasn't going to waste a lifetime of experience—he had a life to lead, things to do, places to go, and he was going to make it all happen by continuing to lead a productive and valuable life.

> How many successful people do you know who have retired and do nothing?
>
>

By this stage there was no holding him back. He was completely sold on the idea of continuing to work and was already back in charge of his own life. It was a wonderful moment as his despondent mood gave way to a new purpose.

He set about expanding and restructuring his practice, and before long Paul was working three days instead of five and making more money than ever. In the process he was training and mentoring young doctors, while providing a vastly improved service for the community. Local tradesmen completed all the home renovations Paul had been planning to do in "retirement," so they felt pretty good about it too. He felt better, everyone felt better.

Paul has his life back and in the has process improved the lot of countless other people. You could argue that you have an economic and communal duty not to retire, but that might be taking ourselves a bit too seriously!

As Paul's story shows, it's all in the mind. Despite being preconditioned for a life of endless endeavor and determined survival, we've been re-programmed into accepting the concept of retirement and its associated withdrawal from active life. We prepare for retirement as a matter of course and actually look forward to the great day, often putting money aside and paying people large fees to look after it for us. And the ultimate irony is that *not* retiring is somehow deemed a sign of failure.

> The ultimate irony is that *not* retiring is somehow deemed a sign of failure.

The cold, hard reality is that retirement can now last for years—and we're talking about twenty or thirty years. In some countries that's two or three life sentences—and, silliest of all, we've sentenced ourselves, then gone voluntarily into home detention. Hard to believe? Just look around you.

We know what you're probably still thinking: "But, I have to retire. Everyone does when they get to sixty or sixty-five."

Says who?

And this is where it gets really interesting—the trite reasons we give ourselves to justify this belief. They revolve around slowing down, coupled with associated decline in health, lack of up-to-date skills, and diminished mental agility.

In other words, people over sixty are worn-out basket-cases who belong out of sight and out of mind in a retirement village before finally being shunted off into the annex for the truly senile.

What's truly amazing about this is that they don't go nuts earlier. This isn't because the good folks running these places are not doing their level best to make it a pleasant experience. But what can you do for someone who has given up hope and is resigned to waiting for the inevitable?

The Japanese have cottoned on to the sheer stupidity of this. Brain games are all the rage in Japan, where older people realize the importance of keeping an active mind. They're flocking to electronic stores to buy games that test their mental agility and keep them bright and alert. Now—no disrespect to the Japanese, whom we value for their culture, their food, and their architecture—but the thought of these fine people sitting around playing games to keep their minds active fills us with dismay.

They're on the right track—it *is* vital to keep our minds active. We now know that the more mentally and physically active you are throughout your life, the less likely you are to develop Alzheimer's. Significantly, it's never too late to start, and one of the best things you can do is read, or anything else that keeps your mind active. By the way, that doesn't include watching television, which is the equivalent of putting your brain into neutral.

It also helps to stay fit; just half an hour of exercise a day can deliver a rewarding oxygen boost to the brain, helping improve your memory and thinking ability. There's even a theory that dancing is the best exercise of all, as it involves both mental and physical agility to keep you on your toes. And that's just the start. Personally, we can't avoid the conclusion that millions of years of evolution were not intended for us to spend our latter years dancing and playing mind games. What a waste that would be.

There is a real danger here of getting bogged down in debate about our purpose in life and why we exist. Learned philosophers from Aristotle to Bertrand Russell have debated this topic endlessly, and seldom got past the stage of answering every question with yet another question.

Speaking for ourselves, we can't accept that we were put on this earth merely to have children and die. That may be true of others in the animal kingdom, but as humans we've evolved to a higher level with a higher purpose. We're not talking any New Age nonsense here; the simple facts are we are an evolving species and we're here to leave more of a legacy than having merely existed. We're here to do something with our lives, to make a difference.

> We're here to do something with our lives, to make a difference.

Remember that feeling you had in your late teens or early twenties when you had your whole life in front of you? Today was for living, with tomorrow just another day, another opportunity? And yesterday, what was that? Who cared?

Your destiny then was to live as if there were no tomorrow. The thought that you might have no future or purpose never crossed your mind. You set out to make your dreams come true, and woe betide anyone who suggested you were good for little more than sitting around doing nothing.

So what changed? How did someone from the retirement police suddenly end up in charge of your life?

In 1948 the novelist George Orwell wrote *1984*, his book about a future where Thought Police controlled everyone's mind. Of course 1984 came and went and we laughingly concluded we'd missed out on the terrible future Orwell predicted, while in reality it was happening all around us. The Thought Police are everywhere, we just don't realize it. Every now and then we spot them, but, just as Orwell predicted, we're quickly persuaded that these frightful people have our interests at heart. Yeah, right!

We willingly sentence ourselves to twenty or thirty years of life in the retirement prison and thank society for its generosity. We stare gratefully into the mirror and fail to see the Thought Police staring back. Not even Orwell could have predicted that we would be the ones to brainwash ourselves. How on earth did it happen?

"Like us to turn off your life support, sir/madam?"

"Oh, yes please, I've lived quite long enough, thank you."

It may well be true that we get the destiny we deserve — but no one deserves *that*.

Businessman Jack Welch couldn't have put it better when he said, "Control your own destiny or someone else will." He was in good, although unlikely, company with the

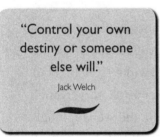

"Control your own destiny or someone else will."

Jack Welch

Chinese military leader Chiang Kai-shek, who said "We write our own destiny . . . we become what we do." And while we're quoting the wise and famous, here's Sir Winston Churchill: "The chain of destiny can only be grasped one link at a time." And if all that is too Establishment for you, consider the words of Bob Marley: "Every man gotta right to decide his own destiny."

We want you to get your life back and enjoy yourself. Decide your own destiny.

Look in the mirror and say after us: "Hooray! I'm alive and I'm going to stay that way and live my life to the fullest.

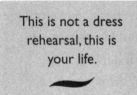

This is not a dress rehearsal, this is your life.

This is not a dress rehearsal, this is it. This is the main event and, as I have the starring role, I'll reserve the right to approve the script and insist on a happy ending."

Key points
to remember

✓ All you have to do is apply a
timetable to your wish list

✓ You've spent your entire life striving
to stay alive—why stop now?

✓ Keep an eye out for the Thought
Police at all times

✓ Take control of your own destiny and
enjoy yourself

9

Work—the sustainable option

Since when was life's journey only about work? You're not a robot. Work should be effort, directed for a purpose—a continuing purpose with no room whatsoever for the notion of retirement.

The sole purpose of this book is to inspire unorthodox, independently-minded, original thinking. If you were to take such an approach to life, do you know what you would be? A heretic. That's right, a heretic. While nowadays it has a connotation of being somehow anti-social, it comes from the Greek word *hairetikos*, meaning "being able to choose." How anti-social is that?

And it's only a few hundred years since heretics were burnt at the stake. Anyone who challenged the status quo, questioned the party line, refused to follow the accepted norm was dubbed a heretic and burnt at the stake. These days they're usually written off as cranks and weirdos and generally ignored.

This includes people who say they have no intention of retiring. First there are those pitying glances. "Ahhhh, so you need to keep working, do you?" This is shorthand for: "So you're a complete failure, are you? Couldn't put enough aside—no pension plan, no investments, a complete loser."

Should you then presume to explain that *retiring* is for losers and you have every intention of living a full and active life, while at the same time doing everything that people who retire do, well, then you're really asking for it. Now comes the tirade about tired old farts desperately hanging on to their youth and denying the next generation their place in the sun. Yes, you'll be made to feel guilty. And if that doesn't have you cringing with shame, there is always the subtle envy approach. "Oh, I'd love to carry on, but I owe it to my wife/husband to spend some time together." What have these people been doing all their lives? Living in separate homes?

Finally, when you've shrugged off these attempts to dissuade you from getting on with your life, they'll start treating you as though you no longer exist—the modern equivalent of burning someone at the stake.

If this concerns you one jot, take heart; they'll be quietly watching from the sidelines, as curiosity always gets the better of them. And when they see how successfully and happily you deal with "living" beyond the age of retirement, they'll soon be banging on your door to learn the secret of your success.

And you can explain how you deleted "retirement" from your vocabulary and redefined the word "work." Life became a work in progress, a continuing experience, and as part of your journey you've transformed yourself from a lemming, hurtling towards the edge of the cliff, and are now positively charging towards new challenges and delights.

> Life is a work in progress, a continuing experience, and as part of your journey you're charging towards new challenges and delights.
>
>

So why is it so important to keep working? Don't we deserve a break from all that? You work to maintain your health and well-being. You work to stay connected in your community, and, most of all, you work to stay "visible." Retire and you effectively cease to exist so far as the rest of the world is concerned.

Nothing better illustrates the benefit of keeping an active mind and staying visible than our friend Dr. Leslie Kay, one of the few people whose name we haven't changed in this book.

During the Cold War, Leslie worked as a scientist for the British Navy, developing underwater sonar technology and using sound waves to find enemy submarines. He went on to become one of the world's leading electrical and electronic engineers, a specialist in sonic devices to help blind people "see."

Bats do it, moths do it, and now, thanks to Leslie, people without sight can do it too—recognize objects using sound. This remarkable man has developed an affordable, effective mobility device that allows the user to hear sounds bouncing off nearby objects.

Dr. Kay was the first person to receive Britain's National Scientific Achievement Award for his *Sonic Torch*, the first commercial electronic device for blind people. Then, as Head of the Electrical Engineering Department at Canterbury University, New Zealand, Dr. Kay further developed his invention and went on to win the $100,000 inaugural global Saatchi & Saatchi Innovation in Communication Award, satisfying the criterion of an innovation that "meets the most needs of the most people."

By now he was well and truly removed from university life and operating from a workshop in his own home. He further fine-tuned his technology, which enables blind people to walk about more freely and, amazingly, in the case of a Japanese boy, to accurately strike a baseball lobbed towards him.

Despite the idea being applauded the world over, and used by blinded war veterans in the United

States, the idea never really took off because of price resistance. But that didn't stop Leslie. Next came a miniaturized low-cost sonar device clipped to a long cane, again sending out harmless ultrasonic waves that bounce back off objects in the blind person's pathway and electronically convert into unique sounds revealing the shape and size of objects. The price dropped dramatically, with his *Sonar-Cane* now selling internationally. Did we mention that by now he was eighty-four and still going strong?

He puts it all down to keeping an active mind and body that you need to keep in good working order to enjoy yourself at *any* stage of life, and even more so when you're debt-free and have more options.

> You need to keep an active mind and body in good working order to enjoy yourself at *any* stage of life.

Yet despite this, huge pressure remains to retire. But we'll continue to be heretics and advise you to keep working and stay connected to life and your community. Keep working and maintain not just an income, but relationships and self-worth. Adopt the attitude and make it happen.

In our research for this book, we interviewed numerous people who specialize in the retirement field, and found that

> With the right attitude you can have a real, meaningful, and mentally enriched life to the very end.

all those who have a fruitful life through the "retirement" years are people with the right attitude. With the right attitude you can have a real, meaningful, and mentally enriched life to the very end.

Retirement is akin to being in a dark hole and, as with every hole, there are several options. Some people are content to rest there. Some wait patiently for someone to lift them out. Some just keep digging, so the hole gets bigger, while others wish they could get out

> There are always options, and options are a real source of genuine power.

but can't seem to find an escape route, constantly searching for a realistic option. This advice is for the latter. Remember: there are always options, and options are a real source of genuine power.

Take Alex. Alex was fifty, on his second marriage with four young children, no assets and no savings. His position was about as bad as it gets. He was beside himself with worry about how he'd manage in retirement, which he thought was just fifteen years away.

Alex was a tradesman, able to work as many hours as he wished, but with all his commitments and new-found responsibilities he found himself hopelessly going around in what appeared to be never-ending circles. Did Alex have choices? Yes, but none of these even started to materialize until he forgot about retirement. Then, and only then, did he realize that no one was going to dig him out of the hole, so he'd better do something about it himself. What Alex needed was some attitude, but we'll come back to him shortly.

Optimism is the secret of a happy life. Of course it helps to have a healthy body, but a healthy and positive mind is equally, if not more, important. And that's where a great attitude to life comes in.

Medical researchers around the world are now practically unanimous that our own self-perception is critical to ageing well. If you have a positive outlook, then life is going to be better, even if you aren't in perfect physical shape.

> Medical researchers agree that if you have a positive outlook, life is going to be better.

As we get older, we come to accept that we might seize up slightly and march to a slightly slower drumbeat—but that doesn't mean we have to feel bad about it. Older people who accept they no longer have the body of a twenty-two-year-old can still have the mind and attitude of a younger person. The elixir of youth is attitude — just think of your hair as silver, not gray. That's the secret.

> The elixir of youth is attitude—just think of your hair as silver, not gray. That's the secret.

Accept the reality of having grown a little older, but also accept that you can still have a life full of joy and expectation. Continue to set targets. Continue to have dreams, a future plan, and a timetable. As we've already discussed, the greatest fear we harbor around this subject is our financial security. That's what drives older people nuts — worrying about their financial wherewithal.

The good news is that a positive attitude to growing older — a determination not to retire and a real will to continue working — quickly removes many of those financial concerns. Refusing to retire gives you enormous financial security and independence. For a start it keeps you in the real world, surrounded by people who are alive and getting on with their lives; making plans, setting targets — just like you.

Another concern people have as they get older is that they will see less and less of their children, often because they remember how they behaved towards their own ageing parents. They remember those dreaded Sunday lunchtime phone calls: "Hello, Mom, how are you? Oh, sorry to hear that. Never mind, keep taking the pills. Yes, we're fine.

Yes, Sarah is doing well at school. Look, sorry about this, Mom, but we have friends coming 'round for lunch. Have to go, look after yourself, call you later . . . 'bye . . . 'bye . . . yes . . . yes . . . 'bye." Click.

Most older people are scared about this happening to them and it's a well-founded fear—there's a growing market in providing paid companionship for the elderly.

The brutal truth is that most adult children can't stand being around their ageing parents because they can be boring and self-obsessed. And this is what their own children think, the caring and loving ones, the ones who should be eternally grateful for everything their parents did for them.

Seriously, though, children look at their ageing parents and quickly realize they're looking in the mirror, seeing a reflection of what's to come. They don't like it, so they turn away.

Think about the older people you know who are constantly surrounded by younger people, in demand and involved with their children and grandchildren; older people who seem to be the center of attention. And what are you looking at? You're looking at people with a twinkle in their bright, alert eyes, people with an obvious zest for life.

Look a bit closer and you'll see that you're also looking at people who are constantly questioning and challenging. These are people who talk about what they're going to do tomorrow, not what they did yesterday, people who can laugh at life's absurdities and, more importantly, laugh at themselves instead of constantly complaining.

These are people who have life as their currency, not age or illness. In short you're looking at interesting older people who are always irresistibly fascinating to younger people, including, but not exclusively, their own children.

They stay in touch with their children but also have a large and vibrant social network and strong personal relationships. Throw in a continuing and active professional or working life and suddenly you're even more interesting and worthwhile.

We've talked about how the notion of retirement came about because of the need to create a space for the younger people coming up behind, and the equal need to keep the existing workers happy with the promise of better things to come. Against this background, the creation of the social welfare state, in its various forms, offered a security blanket in retirement. However, as we've also seen, the welfare state is facing collapse, requiring a total rethink of how we approach and deal with an ageing population.

This isn't peculiar to the West; other cultures have dealt with ageing in their own way. Throughout Asia and the Pacific Islands young people are brought up to respect older people, another form of social welfare. Encourage your children to respect the elderly and they will in turn be there to look after you in your old age.

Or you can start looking after yourself, which brings us back to Alex the tradesman.

Alex needed to build his business, and to do that he needed to adopt a positive attitude. He started by hiring younger tradesmen to do the heavy work on a job-by-job basis, while he concentrated on managing, supervising, and bringing in new business. He created a business he could drive well past the conventional retirement age. Alex had his foot on the bottom rung of the ladder out of the dark hole of retirement.

You'd be astonished by how quickly someone like Alex can climb all the way out and into the fresh air and daylight that surrounds everyone with a purpose, a future, and a positive attitude. Much better than existing on a state-promised pittance that probably won't be there in the near future. Change how you think—that's the trick.

And change is essential. Change is good for us; it stimulates and fires up new brain patterns. And that's very important, as we now know an active mind is capable of making new brain cells, albeit at a slower rate.

> Change is good for us; it stimulates and fires up new brain patterns.

When Edith hit her fifties, harsh reality dawned.
A recently widowed teacher with two dependent
children, she was facing raising a family on her own
with the prospect of enforced retirement when she
reached sixty. A math teacher, Edith quickly calculated
she would need more than her government pension
to get by. It was time to take stock of her assets, and
on the face of it she had precious little.

However, the house had been paid for by her late
husband's insurance, and it had a reasonably large
garden. This set Edith to wondering what she could
do other than teach. First, there was her lifelong love
of plants—to say Edith had a green thumb would be
an understatement. She didn't hesitate, and began
nursing seedlings and cuttings from her garden, and
before long her Saturday morning stall was attracting
neighbors and passers-by. Not only were they buying
her produce, they were asking for advice and then
engaging her services as a garden designer.

Edith read every book there was to be had on
garden landscaping and plants and began wondering
if she could perhaps write her own book. She
could—and it sold far and wide, winning her several
literary prizes. Somewhere along the way, retirement

from teaching came and went unnoticed. What began with a few potted plants had developed into a full-scale native plant nursery and landscaping consultancy. There was also a flourishing trade in fresh organic eggs, thanks to the chickens that roamed her garden.

She was making headlines, too, climbing an ancient tree as part of a protest against development in her area. The headline writers were rather taken with the fact that by then Edith was a sprightly seventy-year-old.

As the years went by, Edith's nursery became a haven for native plants, prompting the town council she had once battled over trees to declare her home and garden a local treasure, purchasing it as a living museum and heritage home, with Edith engaged to maintain it for as long as she chose. At the time of writing she was still going strong, at the age of ninety-one, with her latest book about to be published, and a children's book underway. All because she'd taken stock of her assets some forty years earlier, decided retirement wasn't an option and created a truly fulfilling life.

Key *points* to remember

✓ Choosing not to retire will invite criticism, so be prepared

✓ Working maintains relationships and self-worth, as well as income

✓ There are always options when you forget about retirement

✓ Optimism is the secret of longevity—accept the reality of growing older, but demand a happy and fulfilling life

✓ Continue to set targets, have dreams and always have a plan for the future

10

How to get your life back

Turning sixty, or sixty-five, is much easier if you've thought it through. What you *don't* do is put a stake in the ground by making it a major event and having the big party. What's the big deal? It's just a year like any other. Treat the big six-oh as a huge yawn. That way sixty comes and goes and nothing changes.

> Treat the big six-oh as a huge yawn. That way sixty comes and goes and nothing changes.

If you *do* have the big party, all everyone will want to know is what you're going to do in your retirement, so avoid the party and you get to avoid all that defeatist nonsense. You also get to avoid all those depressing people who think sixty is the end of life as we know it. Accept that sixty or sixty-five is no cause for any demarcation, let alone celebration. No drawing a line in the sand.

By taking this simple step and adopting a positive attitude, you're already out in front and diminishing the negativity of "age." Think of it like this. Before enlighten-ment—*perspiration*. After enlightenment—*inspiration*.

To succeed in a life without retirement, it is essential that you learn to think strategically, which means not just having an objective, but a strategy to make it happen.

Far too many people, companies, and organizations make the same mistake of confusing an objective with a strategy. You really would be amazed at the number of companies we deal with, run by smart, intelligent people, who do just that. Seeking success, they will typically and rather grandly scribble the words "improved customer relations" on the whiteboard at their weekend retreat, then go home, thinking they have a strategy. All they *have* is an objective of improved customer relations, when what they *need* is a strategy to achieve improved customer relations. Don't get us wrong, they'll try very hard to be nice to everyone but, without that missing link, without the actual strategy, it will be very much a hit-and-miss affair.

It all comes down to developing an objective and then a strategy to make it a reality. Remember what we said earlier about wish lists and dreams? What makes your dream a reality is to give it a timetable. Or to put it another way, the left-brain enactment to the right-brain wistfulness. You've engaged the "gift," now get the "servant" to work.

> What makes your dream a reality is to give it a timetable.

Your objective is to keep on living a worthwhile life, well past the age when everyone else is retiring. That's a great objective. Now, we're going to help you develop a strategy to make that not only possible, but a reality. Think of it as a road map to reach your goal.

Step one:
Plan to be debt-free

The first step, and it's an important one, is to plan to be debt-free. Working most of your life and paying interest on your debts may have seemed a good idea in the bad old days before enlightenment, but why continue? And don't get sucked into providing a debt-free capital base for your children. Why on earth should you fund them into a lifestyle they can't afford, and risk your own financial security?

There's an old Chinese saying: "A journey of a thousand miles begins with the first step." It doesn't say: "A journey of a thousand miles begins at the 800-mile mark, if you ride on your parents' back."

You honor your children more by allowing them to make their own way in life, not by steering them in a direction you select and finance. Philosophers often refer to children as "arrows" that leave their parents' bow. None of them refers to arrows with strings attached.

Thinking smart should be the order of the day, and still having debt when you're trying to get a better balance in your life simply doesn't make sense. Debt puts you on an interest-driven treadmill, and there's no fun to

> Still having debt when you're trying to get a better balance in your life simply doesn't make sense.

be had on the "bigger, better, brighter treadmill" that demands the newest and most expensive of everything, if it means lying awake at night, worrying about how to pay for it.

From this moment forward you should focus on everything in your life being more functional and affordable. Step back and observe how the debt treadmill has a nasty habit of getting out of control, with the real sequence of events more like "bigger, better, brighter, boom, *bust*." We'd all rather ignore the bust bit, which is usually the signal to start all over again.

Bigger house, bigger mortgage, flashier car—these are the main drivers for most people, who simply accumulate more debt to pay for them, a self-consuming and ultimately destructive pathway.

Nothing sums this up better than the definition of the word "mortgage" which derives from two Latin words, *mort* and *gage*, meaning "death" and "pledge." We'll leave you to draw your own conclusions. The first thing you should do is put your new-found attitude to work—getting rid of the mortgage. Why on earth would you want to keep increasing your death pledges?

We're all for being competitive, but can see no sense whatsoever in this futile race life has become for so many of our contemporaries, whose sole objective seems to be reaching the finish line with maximum assets, even if they're loaded with debt. We really can't see the sense in that.

To help you with this first step, here's a useful tip: stop buying things you don't need. Why do you keep buying new stuff? Determine that from now on you will always challenge every major purchase decision with these questions:

- Is it for me and do I really need it?

- What will it achieve that's different and better than I already have?

- Am I buying this simply to impress my neighbors and friends?

- How important is that?

- Am I buying it because I have nothing better to do?

Thirty years ago Michael decided to build himself a retirement home. Sadly he'd accepted the conventional attitude, but at least he was thinking ahead.

The first thing he did was withdraw all his retirement savings and put them into a plot of land by the beach. Not the most popular beach, but a beach all the same. That done, he couldn't afford to build on it, but he had an architect design a tasteful home that would one day blend effortlessly into the beach landscape. Five years later he had enough money to build the double garage. He parked his boat in one side, converting the other half into living space for himself and his family to use at weekends.

We watched all this with some interest and, when we asked how he was getting on, Michael replied, "I think I've died and gone to heaven. Do you know I can lie in bed and look at my boat! It can't get any better than that." A few years later Michael completed the house.

By now Michael was starting to listen as we talked about our ideas on the futility of playing the retirement game. In the bad old days, when "retirement" featured in his life, Michael would have thought of selling the city house, putting the money in the bank and living off the interest at his beach home. Not any more—and now, as a complete bonus, that beach house is a valuable asset to enjoy. He's cleared his debts and no longer buys "stuff" for the sake of it or to impress the neighbors.

And is he thinking of retiring? Heavens no. Michael's beach home is no longer an endpoint or an escape hatch, it is now just part of an active and rewarding lifestyle. He has an open mind and will do anything, part- or full-time, to maintain his current lifestyle and state of mind. And is Michael some high-flying lawyer or businessman? No. Michael is as down-to-earth as they come.

Several of our colleagues have also cottoned on, and have stopped buying bigger and more expensive houses and cars, involving bigger debts. They've learned to be satisfied with what they have, and are pleasantly surprised to discover they now have a *disposable* income, often for the first time in their lives.

> Be satisfied with what you have and discover you have a *disposable* income.

They can have holidays and work less, selectively doing only what they enjoy, because they don't have a bank manager hovering over them with one hand out and a stick in the other.

Don't get us wrong. Debt has a very valuable place in our society, but it's a bit like a boat made of ice. You use it for a purpose, to get from A to B and then you get out. Otherwise, to state the obvious, like any boat made of ice, it'll sink and you'll go down with it.

Step two:
Make and nurture good relationships

OK—that's finance sorted, so on to the next step in our strategy. Embrace good friends and relationships. Not the ones allied to your wealth or position, but the ones with people who'll be there for you when the chips are down. With good friends, real friends, nothing will change, regardless of your age or theirs.

And keep making new friends, of all ages. If your friends are linked to your job or the position you hold, when that changes, so might they. Instead of being a non-event, age will become an occasion of loss. Not many people truly want to live in isolation, and the way to avoid this is to invest time with your friends and those you wish to befriend. You'll no doubt have enough obligation-type relationships with family and extended family. Some of these will be rewarding, while others may be a considerable strain. To be blunt, if experience is anything to go by, a few may even be a right royal pain in the proverbial. As they say, you can choose your friends but you can't choose your family, so the secret is to choose your friends well.

Step three:
Undertake regular maintenance and repairs

You should aim to arrive in your sixties with all the elements of good health in as perfect order as you can get. Keep up with all the running health repair and maintenance programs, just as you would on your car. Need your teeth fixed? Do it. Need new glasses? Get them. Need some other body part refurbished? Have it done.

We tend to maintain our material assets yet take for granted the most important—ourselves. You have your car regularly serviced, but are you having yourself checked out just as often?

Operations of any kind are easier on the body and the wallet the younger you are. In fact, in later years the biggest single risk from operations can be from the general anesthetic that causes your brain process to shut down and which needs to be able to reboot, rather like a computer, when the power goes back on. So keep up the physical maintenance program, and if you don't have one already don't waste any more valuable time; start right now.

> You have your car regularly serviced, but are you having yourself checked out just as often?

We're not suggesting it's easy. We know what goes through your mind. You're turning sixty, what do you do? Increase the private health cover? Panic? Give up? All of these thoughts are likely to flood through your mind. Maintain all your assets, material and otherwise, and you can really afford to junk the retirement virus and get on with your life.

There are no end of people out there prepared to ensure that turning sixty can be a pretty traumatic experience. You know you've reached the dreaded milestone when your private health provider sends a timely reminder, a kindly yet detailed letter, proclaiming you're now entering a new age and risk group, and consequently your premiums are going to increase.

You take out these policies when you're young, thinking you'll need them when you get older, as indeed you probably will. What the insurers don't explain is that when you do get older you won't be able to afford them, so it's a self-defeating policy. Pun intended.

Pity you can't put an old head on young shoulders . . . or perhaps you can.

Faced with the dilemma of continually rising health premiums, Sandra and Ken did a cost-benefit analysis and concluded, whichever way they looked at it, that they were on the losing end. Then they had a bright idea. They turned the entire equation on its head with the simple question: "Why plan to be old and sick?" Why not plan to stay young*ish* and healthy, and avoid the anticipated and seemingly normal physical collapse?

They worked out what could be saved by lowering their premiums to a basic hospital plan and with the balance bought two bicycles. They found cycling such a pleasure that the standard bikes were quickly traded in for better ones, at which point the cycling took on a more serious note. They increased the Sunday morning distance from 6 miles to 12 miles, then gradually all the way to 60 miles. Then they got competitive.

Their first big cycle race was a leg-sapping 100-mile mountain race they finished in under eight hours. Twelve months later they did the same event in six hours, and the following year, on newer, faster bicycles, they cracked the five-and-a-half-hour mark. Was it worth the change? Absolutely.

They've never been fitter and life's challenges don't seem so daunting. What's more—and this is crucially important—their work efficiency has improved enormously. What started out as a simple exercise to rearrange their health cover has brought a whole new dimension to their lives. Boy, have they got their lives back! And there's a deliciously ironic twist. With petrol prices soaring, Ken took to riding to work—not only is he fitter than ever, he now has a tax-deductible company bicycle parked outside his office. Their lives just keep getting better. More to the point; they no longer look back but look forward with pleasure at the long road ahead.

Here's another example of what we're talking about.

Donald was sixty going on eighty when he was given a very simple message from a specialist he was consulting about his increasing stress levels: "I can tell you with some confidence that you will shortly achieve what you've been working really hard towards all these years." Donald briefly thought things might not have been as bad as he imagined, until the specialist continued: "Your stress levels will kill you, but don't worry, you won't feel a thing. It will all be over in less than a minute." There then followed a brief lecture along the lines of, "I've met your type before. There's no point in telling you to slow down and get some balance in your life, so just keep it up. The end isn't far away. Any day now. Next," he called to his nurse.

That was the shock Donald needed. He'd always wanted to go to Peru and see Machu Picchu, and for the past ten years he'd had a picture of it on his desk. It was going to be the first thing he did when he retired.

Machu Picchu is the legendary Lost City of the Andes and, without doubt, one of the world's most impressive archaeological sites. Built by the Incas, it sits on a mountain site of extraordinary beauty, more than 7,000 feet above sea level, in the middle of a tropical mountain forest. Covering some three square miles, it was built in the mid-1400s and was home to some 1000 people, along with their priests and magnificent temples. It is considered the most amazing urban creation of the Inca Empire.

Donald canceled his appointments for the next month, and within days was off to Peru with his friend Greg. The first thing he noticed was that color returned to his previously black-and-white life, along with much-needed balance, not to mention a sense of humor.

When they came to the base of the mountain they hauled on their hiking boots and set off. Altitude sickness was a whole new experience, and one that Donald hadn't banked on, but chewing a mixture of coca leaves and sniffing a type of peppermint plant seemed to help.

Donald saw things he'd never imagined, including a visit to a centuries-old hospice built by the Incas. The site was surrounded by small stone-enclosed herb gardens and looked out over a magnificent valley. The Incas had a drive for work, and they certainly knew how to look after their sick and dying. But the real eye-opener was that they never retired.

From that point Donald's life was never going to be the same. He'd taken a month off and turned his back on the prospect of an early and sudden death, thanks to a walk in the mountains. We can't all be fortunate enough to have a doctor as smart as Donald's, but we can read the warning signs. Donald, by the way, is now sixty going on forty.

You don't have to travel halfway around the world or climb a mountain to make the change. Join a gym or a club, engage in activities that involve mixing with a wide range of people. And remain positive, which includes avoiding negative people like the plague; stick with people who see the glass as half full, not half empty.

> Remain positive, which includes avoiding negative people like the plague.

Step four:
Challenge yourself constantly

To prepare for the next stage of your active life, take on new challenges and take risks, stretching your limits and your horizons. Kick your shoes off and walk barefoot in that great park called "life." That's what all the people we've been telling you about have done, and it's worked for them.

Already we can hear people saying, "but that could be risky," and so it may be, but so is the air most of us breathe and to date we haven't heard anyone suggesting we should stop breathing. That said, we've been convinced to pay more per liter for bottled water than we pay for gasoline. Marketing is a truly wonderful thing. Selling sand to the Arabs or ice to the Eskimos used to be the mark of a super salesman, but that's got nothing on selling overpriced bottled water to people who have perfectly safe drinking water coming out of their taps. It's the "perception is reality" argument all over again.

Step five:
Plan intelligently

Start planning now for an occupation that doesn't have a *use-by* date. Be sensible about this and take a cold, hard look at what you're doing and where you're going. If it's nowhere fast, then you have some work to do. If you need to retrain, do it now and make it a work in progress. Make the transitions in your life as seamless as possible, so they become a continuous part of your daily routine.

> Start planning now for an occupation that doesn't have a *use-by* date.

And here's another useful tip—the answer is probably staring you in the face. Look to your friends. What are they doing? See what's worked for them and follow those paths that you know will work for you.

A Chinese proverb says, "If you're looking for gold, ask someone who's found it." After all, it's pointless asking someone who's also looking—they don't have the answer any more than you do.

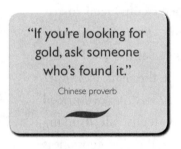

"If you're looking for gold, ask someone who's found it."

Chinese proverb

Beware, however. The world is full of consultants and advisors who profess to know what's best for you, yet their own lives are a shambles. Often of course, the gold they're looking for is yours; all they have to do is part you from it. The first thing we ask any financial adviser or consultant is: "Tell us about your financial position. Are you successful? Are you rich?" And we don't take their word for it. We check them out. Thoroughly.

We tend to follow the advice of Sun Tzu in his book *The Art of War* where he says "If you're going into foreign territory, take a guide." The secret to all success lies in seeking advice from people who have demonstrably proven they know the answer. Someone who has been successful in the same field is someone with the strategy to help you achieve your goal.

Keep your sixth sense engaged; it's your intuition that will guide you through a maze of unchartered territory. And embrace change. Accept the things you can't change, don't hark back to the good old days, just get on with living for today. As Kahil Gibran put it, "Everyone stands in the sun, but some stand with their backs to it and all they see is their shadow." If that's what you're doing, then for heaven's sake turn around, face the sun, and give everyone a break.

Step six:
Keep smiling

The last step is a small but vital one. Whatever else you decide to do, keep your sense of humor at all costs. Humor is the lightning rod to sanity, and it's been said

> Humor is the lightning rod to sanity.

that God gave man a sense of humor to compensate for his rational brain. It's certainly a good way to calm down a tense and difficult situation, and if you have an ability to laugh at yourself, then life becomes so much easier. They don't say laughter is the best medicine for nothing!

So, there's a strategy—now it's up to you to use the ideas we've suggested to customize it to fit your plans and dreams. Remember, you're genetically geared to survive. Relax and let your intuition guide you. You *know* who you are, just don't let anyone talk you out of it.

Key points to remember

✓ Plan to be debt-free and stop buying unnecessary stuff

✓ Make and nurture good relationships

✓ Keep up your personal maintenance

✓ Challenge yourself constantly

✓ Plan ahead intelligently—look for an occupation without a use-by date

✓ Keep your sense of humor at all costs

11
Live the dream

How often have you heard yourself say, "if only?"

- If only I had the time.

- If only I'd won the lottery.

- If only the children were settled or financially stable.

- If only I could afford it.

It's the typical daydream of someone blinded by the whole retirement business. "If only . . ." tends to be associated with a dream, a pleasant daydream, but a dream all the same. While everyone from Aristotle to Sigmund Freud has theorized about why we dream, the truth is no one really knows. But here's our favorite option—we like it because it makes sense to us.

When we're awake, billions of brain cells go about their daily business and ensure that all our necessary bodily functions, such as pumping blood and breathing, continue. Dreams are thought to fulfil this function while we are asleep, and are in fact our brain cells exercising. Dreams are also believed to be a reflection of unfinished business and concerns from the day.

This is where Freud comes in with his belief that dreams carry our hidden desires, while others argue that dreaming is our way of either storing or dumping the vast array of information gained during the day. We'll never really know.

Daydreaming is different. This involves the right or creative side of the brain being used to visualize a dream scenario of what we might like to do. You don't need us to tell you the most common daydreams revolve around love or lust, but daydreams are very important, because they can also help us plan a wish list.

And here's the rub. Wishing can be a dangerous game, as all too often you get what you wish for. As a popular song of our youth reminds us—"Watch out! You might get what you're after!" This tends not to apply to winning the lottery, but wish for retirement and you'll certainly get it.

Daydream by all means, but dream of a positive and rewarding future. We call this "active meditation," a form of controlled role-playing, as you map out your needs and how they can be achieved. You get to write the plot of your dreams and then play it out, first in your mind and

> Active meditation helps you map out your needs and how they can be achieved.

then in reality. That's the trick to making your dreams come true.

Dreams can become a reality if they have a well-thought-out timetable and strategy. If at first you don't succeed, change the plot and play it out again. This is where your inner voice comes into play, helping you to assess your options. Instantly stop any daydream that looks backwards or has a negative connotation. You *only* go forward. You are *always* positive. Make that the rule for daydreaming and it will quickly become your reality.

> Dreams can become a reality if they have a well-thought-out timetable and strategy. If at first you don't succeed, change the plot and play it out again.

Sports people call it "visualization." They visualize the race or the game, every step of the way, as it encourages a positive outcome. To see this in action, watch a high-jumper prepare for take-off. It works just as well for a game of football and equally well for life itself.

Of course, you have to be careful not to confuse daydreaming with fantasy. The whole purpose is to fulfill a dream, so your daydream is a work in progress—think of it as a strategy-planning session if you prefer.

And if you won't do it for the sake of your sanity, then do it for the money.

Only the truly delusional are waiting for the government

> Only the truly delusional are waiting for the government to take care of them.

to take care of them. "Social welfare," "social security," call it what you will, is history. The generous refer to an uncertain future, while the pragmatists and realists have accepted state care of the elderly is a dead duck. As we've already seen, most countries are woefully ill-prepared to cope with what is becoming progressively unsustainable, as there are too many "oldies" and not enough "youngies" to support them.

Every economist in the world will tell you the tax base will not be able to cope. Baby boomers have had it lucky all their lives; their parents prospered in the post-war years and produced a generation that both believed and proved it could achieve whatever it chose.

These are the people who invented the Pill, free love, and women's lib, in that order. These were the protest generation, who made love not war. "Never mind what about, just protest, man!" They were born into an era of remarkable economic prosperity that was essentially worry-free. Consumerism was their way of life. They didn't just own the washing machines and telephones their parents dreamed of, they owned their own cars, their own homes. They wanted it, they had it. This was the "me" generation, and because of their numerical significance their attitude to everything from technology to sex to wearing jeans is surveyed, charted, and pored over by academics and popular columnists alike.

Some gurus have gone so far as to suggest these folk will be teenagers at heart until the day they die. But, what's interesting about all these theories is the assumption all baby boomers belong in one great graying mass. Nonsense.

They range from parents of tiny children to grand- or even great-grandparents. They may be hugely successful and rich, or merely successful in their chosen way of life. One thing is certain, though, they are almost all united in their determination not to grow old, while our social and economic system is still demanding that they get off the treadmill and retire. Imagine the confusion for someone still running marathons and going to the gym being told they're past it and must give up their desk job. It's madness. It's ironic too, that canny marketers and advertisers have cottoned on to the fact that if they want to sell anything to a baby boomer nudging sixty, they have to speak to them in exactly the same terms as they did when they were nudging thirty.

This is a generation that refuses to grow up, let alone grow old, a generation that has hocked itself up to its eyeballs, with debts to pay for those new homes and cars and holidays. Now that they're being told they have to retire, they are, in many cases, frightened at the prospect, as they don't have the resources to continue supporting themselves in the manner to which they have so happily become accustomed.

Is this starting to sound a tad familiar?

Already, there are plans afoot for the good folk of Britain to work till they're sixty-eight before receiving a pension linked to wages and then means-tested, and it's a promise politicians the world over are making. It cunningly allows them to appear generous at the ballot box, while relying on the "get out" clause in the small print—usually along the lines of "should the fiscal situation allow." Anyone with half a brain knows full well it won't.

We baby boomers must accept that we'll have to take responsibility for ourselves. Our parents were rather grandly known as the Greatest Generation, and conditioned to the promise of a pension both from their employer— usually their lifelong employer— and the government.

> We baby boomers must accept that we'll have to take responsibility for ourselves.

They might have been the Greatest Generation, but we're the best educated, and we certainly haven't bought into the notion of holding down one job for life. We go wherever the fancy, the opportunity, the excitement, and the money takes us.

Isn't it odd, then, that so many of us still buy into the idea of retirement? Well, not quite everyone.

Meet inspirational Tina, a fiercely independent single woman who successfully applied for a job as a courtroom typist. Everything was going well until, on her third day at work, she had to fill in a health insurance form. The office manager came rushing over to tell her she'd made a mistake on the form: "This makes you seventy-five years old!" The only mistake Tina had made was filling in her date of birth. As retirement age for courtroom typists was fifty-five, Tina's new job was over before it started.

Not to worry. Tina purchased an old house with seven bedrooms so she could take in student boarders. The venture was so successful she began excavating the basement to create even more bedrooms. At the age of eighty she began dismantling the chimney that was at risk of falling over. Neighbors were astonished to see her clambering around on the roof with her little wicker basket, removing bricks, two or three at a time. Did she discard them? Heavens no, she used them to create an extra car-parking space and a path around the side of the house. The renovated home was then sold.

So where next? A retirement home? A tiny apartment?

Tina used her funds to buy a run-down cottage on land big enough for another home. She then lived in the cottage while building a new house. And when we say she built it, we mean just that.

Allowing for her age, she accepted she could no longer do the heavy work any more, so she bought a semi-completed "shell" from the local technical institute where carpentry students had built the home as part of their training. All she had to do was arrange the necessary permits to have the house moved onto site, and have it wired and painted and plumbed. Then she sanded the floors and moved in her furniture.

While all this was going on, she arranged the flower garden, the vegetable garden, and planted fruit trees. Anywhere Tina lived was always a blaze of color with flowers, fresh vegetables, and fruit—food for body and soul, for her friends and family alike.

It's easy to see how she was such an inspirational person in so many people's lives. She never accepted the words "no" or "impossible" and certainly not "retire." Education was a lifelong driver for Tina and at age eighty-nine she moved again, to be in walking distance of a technical institute so she could attend night classes. And what gave her such an indefatigable energy for life? She simply believed in living each day to the fullest. She never accepted at any stage that she was "past it." Certainly, she needed to constantly think smarter to overcome life's hurdles. And she did!

Mike and Marie were in real danger of being permanent retirees. They'd both stopped working and bought a small home close to their children and grandchildren. The end had come. There they were, little more than glorified babysitters. It was about as bad as it could get until Mike and Marie asked themselves the fundamental question: Why were they giving up? Why not change towns, move to an environment that was stimulating and take on new challenges?

Mike and Marie bought a home with a wonderful mountain view and big enough for all their family to come and stay. But what about all that space when the family wasn't there? They put up a "Bed & Breakfast" sign and soon their first guests started arriving. They set up a website and the bookings flooded in, as did the referrals from their happy and satisfied customers, and Mike bought a small boat to take guests out fishing on the nearby lake.

Now they're so busy their family has to book, to ensure there'll be room for them when they arrive. Mike and Marie are in their late sixties but look younger than ever. They have their lives back and life has a purpose for them again as they've become a vital part of their new community. They're back in demand, not as child or house minders, but for themselves and what they have to offer. Already they're talking about an overseas trip to celebrate, and get away from it all, but just for a while. Had they stayed where they were, they'd be no more than aged grandparents waiting for the inevitable.

Mike and Marie have clearly demonstrated that it's never too late. Even if you've given up, take a deep breath and start again.

> Find a guide, not an adviser or consultant; and don't risk your financial assets on someone else's dream.

Just a word of caution. When you're looking for new business ventures, or some scheme or other to be involved in, remember the old adage: "If it looks too good to be true, then it probably is." Remember also to find a guide, not an adviser or consultant; and don't risk your financial assets on someone else's dream. If you're looking to go into a new venture, make sure that you:

- Don't go into debt

- Don't commit to a lease or other contract that has long-term or punitive exit clauses.

- Stick to a business you can manage well within your existing skill base.

- Ensure you can walk away if it doesn't work out.

- *Don't* mortgage your house to fund the venture.

- Remember you're going into it for fun and profit, not stress and depression. If a risk is called for, then only risk an amount you are (happily, or even unhappily) prepared to lose.

It also helps to remember that where and how you live should be a philosophical decision, not a financial one. Choose where you will live for lifestyle reasons, because that's where you want to be, not because you may or may not make money on the deal. Any financial profit should be treated for what it is: a bonus.

> Where and how you live should be a philosophical decision, not a financial one.

Time and time again we meet people looking to sell their home to keep moving up the social and financial ladder. No sooner are they able to manage the mortgage on their current home than they seek to buy a bigger, brighter one and, of course, take on more debt. In other words, back to the treadmill, going nowhere, only faster.

Money is always a burning issue. The big question around the world's dinner tables right now is "How much do you need to save for retirement?" Well, you can forget about how much may be needed, the harsh reality is that most people are saving less than 1 percent of their disposable income. And that's everywhere, worldwide.

Millions of people around the globe are about to put up the "retired" sign and, with nothing in the bank, are praying the social security check will land on their front doormat. They're pinning their hopes on the chance that somehow the creaking and groaning social security system will magically last long enough to see them to their grave.

Oh dear. We do hope that by now you're not one of them. That's why so many people go through life mouthing the "if only" mantra, dreaming of a better life but failing to grasp the essential truth.

Have the dream by all means, but wake up and live it now.

> The harsh reality is that most people are saving less than 1 percent of their disposable income. And that's everywhere, worldwide.

> Have the dream by all means, but wake up and live it now.

Key points to remember

✓ Use your daydreams to plan your wish list

✓ Accept that you'll have to take financial responsibility for the rest of your life

✓ It's never too late to change

✓ If it looks too good to be true, then it probably is

✓ Wake up and start living your dream now

12

Join the retirement revolution

By 2010, nearly one in three workers in the United States will be over the age of fifty. The figure is scarily similar right around the developed world.

As the relative proportion of younger workers declines, attracting and retaining experienced and reliable workers is becoming a core business strategy for all employers.

> As the relative proportion of younger workers declines, attracting and retaining experienced and reliable workers is becoming a core business strategy for all employers.

For any company, anywhere in the world, to maintain its competitive edge in the global economy, it must learn to attract older workers. In England, 60 percent of employers consider their business is being held back through a lack of properly experienced or qualified staff. Think about it—more than half the firms in England stymied because they can't get the staff they so desperately need. And that's symptomatic of a worldwide problem.

With millions of baby boomers reaching their sixties, we're staring the answer in the face. Right now we should be planning on how to capitalize on all that wisdom and knowledge and skill to expand our economies. So you can stop worrying about whether there's a future out there for you—the reality is, there isn't a future without you.

Without wishing to bore you with statistics, consider this. Research by a leading bank has found well over 60 percent of people want to work in some fashion after they retire, be it in full- or part-time employment. But there's a sting in the tail. Questioned further, these people admitted their desire to keep working was based entirely on need—they didn't *want* to keep working, they *needed* to. The vast majority of those surveyed still wanted to retire in their late fifties and early sixties, but with some form of ongoing employment because they needed the money.

They talked to the researchers about wanting some form of mental stimulation, something meaningful to do, but the bottom line was they needed to keep working because they needed the money.

> We're brighter, stronger, fitter, and living longer than ever, yet we're still collectively buying into the idea of stopping work somewhere between fifty-five and sixty-five.

By the year 2030, which is only a couple of decades away, there will be 324,000 people over the age of 100 living in the United States. Don't take our word for it; that's the taxman's estimate, and a 431 percent increase on today. And it's not just in the United

States, longevity is becoming a worldwide phenomenon. We're brighter, stronger, fitter, and living longer than ever, yet we're still collectively buying into the idea of stopping work somewhere between fifty-five and sixty-five.

Few economies are able to support their ageing population, even in the short- to medium-term, but imagine what a difference it would make if these people turned their backs on retirement and all kept contributing. Not only would it reduce the burden on the national account, but it would have a positive effect through increased productivity and a vastly increased tax take from this hugely enlarged workforce. Now, if that isn't a win–win situation, then what is?

It is *so* simple. Let's put those depressing statistics to one side and focus on the positive news: that so many employers are starting to recognize what valuable assets the older or senior workers can be.

It's not just your knowledge, experience, and skill that make you hot property, it's the fact that you're in better shape than any generation before you. You have the same energy and drive you had twenty, even thirty years ago. Why on earth would you want to waste such fantastic assets?

> You have the same energy and drive you had twenty, even thirty years ago. Why on earth would you want to waste such fantastic assets?

Continuing to work is now a real option. Indeed, as we have seen, for many economies it's going to be a necessity. You'll be needed more than ever before for the multi-faceted advantages you can provide.

Allow us to repeat an earlier observation. We live in a hi-tech world that allows us to keep going far longer than our ancestors did. There's no longer any requirement to buy into the argument that you need to retire, let alone struggle to make ends meet. If you make the decision to continue working, you'll be in a truly powerful position.

The bywords for the new generation of people working past retirement around the globe are "experienced," "smarter," and "more productive." Once dismissed as economic millstones around the neck of society, they are increasingly viewed as an asset.

> You are now recognized as a viable and valued asset, rather than an irritating statistic in the retirement column. So pick up the ball and run with it.

That's you they're talking about. You are now recognized as a viable and valued asset, rather than an irritating statistic in the retirement column. So pick up the ball and run with it.

Have you noticed that elderly professionals are readily accepted? In fact, sometimes the older the better, on the basis that the older they are, the more they know.

And the word is spreading, with growing recognition that not only does society need to keep all that experience and wisdom in the workplace, but these "oldies" are fitter than ever and have a work ethic second to none. What's more, there are near-invisible hearing aids and even medication to improve memory. There's nothing to stop the boomers working well into their seventies and beyond.

The predicted doomsday when the baby boomers hit sixty and place unbearable strain on the generation coming up behind won't happen if the boomers ignore the nonsense and get on with their lives, which will require a major mind shift.

The surveys seem to concur that older workers are better communicators, and the over-fifties are taking to the Internet quicker than any other age group. The older workforce can also relate better to the customer base which, surprise, surprise, is also getting older. They take fewer sick days than younger employees and are a darn sight more loyal. It's certainly not cheaper, or necessarily more productive, to replace an older employee with a younger, seemingly more energetic one. They just make mistakes faster.

For a glimpse of what the world will soon be like, look no further than the United Kingdom, where within the coming decade 40 percent of the labor force will be aged forty-five or over. By 2010, a fifth of all workers will be older than fifty-five, and already firms are starting to report skill shortages. The answer? Hire unskilled young people or retain and retrain the oldies. Remember too, older workers bring valuable experience and can act as mentors to younger staff.

That's what's coming, so be ready for it.

Such is the demand for good workers, employers are starting to make major concessions that include three-day weeks and much longer holidays, as much as several months, to both retain and attract this valuable resource.

According to the experts—the people who study the facts and make the projections—unemployment should remain low in the developed world, with major competition for skilled people. No one will be able to afford to ignore the experienced, older workers.

> No one will be able to afford to ignore the experienced, older workers.

Yet, despite the urgent need, Americans, who are now living longer, are also retiring earlier than ever before. In the past sixty years, the life expectancy for men and women has increased by between three and four years, but the average age of retirement has dropped three years to sixty-two.

To get a fix on how serious this is, in thirty years 20 percent of the US population will be sixty-five or older. When the bulk of baby boomers reach retirement age, there will be just three workers to every retired person.

Apologies again for all the figures, but they just go to prove there is someone out there who really needs you, even if they don't know it quite yet.

Alan Greenspan, at the age of eighty, stepped down as the US Federal Reserve chairman. Forecasting that older workers could be crucial to economic prosperity, he opened his own economic consulting business with offices in Washington. This is the same man who has warned that as the baby boom generation starts claiming social security retirement benefits it will be impossible to fund such payments with existing tax rates, setting in motion what he has forecast will be "an unsustainable dynamic in which large deficits result in growing interest payments that augment deficits in future years." The consequence of this will have "destabilizing effects" on the economy. In plain English, it'll be a bit like watching a train crash in slow motion.

And the message is getting through. The trend has begun to reverse, albeit slightly. More and more companies are recognizing that the future lies in keeping their existing workers productive.

> The future lies in keeping existing workers productive.

There are fewer replacement workers coming up behind to replace the current workforce, and the future of our economies and our standard of living is becoming more and more dependent on people who would once have been considered "retirees."

But no one should take being able to work on for granted. Some companies will solve the problem by getting smarter with the technology they employ; some will simply retrench on the grounds that a shrinking workforce means a shrinking overall market; others will set up shop in the third world to exploit cheap labor.

A constant worry for employers is the health of this ageing workforce. The last thing they want is to be stuck with massive health insurance bills or have great swathes of a creaking and groaning workforce away on sick leave. The solution will probably lie in using part-timers, and there's something to be said for that. Without having to worry about health costs, holidays, and lay offs, employers can and should pay more when they do need you.

But—there is always a "but"—they'll be looking not just for the smart ones, but for the fit and healthy ones. Just the sort of person you would be looking for if you were doing the employing.

Because we're living longer, and are healthier and wealthier, 75 percent of baby boomers over the age of sixty-five think they're in fine shape. Feeling good is a state of mind, with the word "old" redefined by the quality of the health care we receive, and the diet and exercise regime we follow. We age more quickly because of the way we live. Change that for the better and we age more slowly.

With all this talk of money, we need to recognize that "life cycle" means what it says. It goes around in a circle; it doesn't have a cliff edge with a sign pronouncing, "Retirement Bluff, All Lemmings Jump Off Here."

Those who jump put their hands on their wallets and wonder if there's enough in the back pocket to give them a soft landing. They're in for a rude awakening.

Key points to remember

✓ There is no future without you—you are an increasingly valuable asset

✓ There will be significant positive economic effects if the baby boomers continue working

✓ Workers past "retirement age" are experienced, smarter, and more productive

✓ It is no longer cheaper and more productive to replace older workers

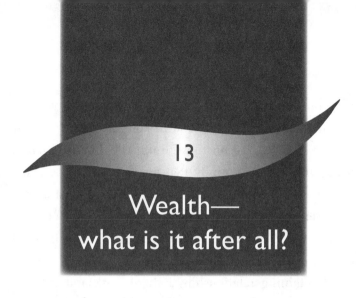

13

Wealth— what is it after all?

Wealth is the sum total of all your assets and these, simply put, are:

- mental and physical health

- wisdom

- knowledge

- experience

- relationships

- property, possessions, and cash

> Once you have your mental and physical health looked after, the next most important item on the list is your relationships.

It is important to recognize that your real wealth is comprised of not only material possessions but also your mental and physical well-being. Once you have your mental and physical health looked after, the next most important item on the list is your relationships, which are vital for keeping you alive, happy, and in control of your life. By relationships, we mean those links with family, friends, work, and the community that enable you to live a life packed with joy, satisfaction, and fulfilment. Just as you need to work to maintain your physical and mental well-being, so you need to work to maintain the full extent of your many different relationships.

Maintaining relationships is hard work and requires an investment of your time. However, you need to invest in *all* of these areas of wealth, not just the material ones, for a full and satisfying life. After all, these assets give you options. The greatest source of power anyone ever has is options—the more options you have, the more power and control you have. And making sure you're in shape to exploit all of those options isn't brain surgery. Eat sensibly, exercise, and sleep.

> The more options you have, the more power and control you have.

Fatigue, the consequence of lack of sleep, combined with a confused body clock, is shaping up as the next big health and safety issue, with major implications on how we all work, be it in the boardroom, emergency clinic, or on the factory floor.

> Adequate sleep is now recognized as being as important as a healthy diet and regular exercise.

Adequate sleep is now recognized as being as important as

a healthy diet and regular exercise. Inadequate sleep impacts on everything we do. It affects our ability to make decisions; the manner and speed with which we react in emergencies; our memory, coordination, and mood. And it's no coincidence that sleep researchers now talk about the "sleep debt" that accumulates with every night you fail to achieve your necessary hours of sleep.

Combine loss of sleep with the time zone changes associated with international travel, and you have the circadian rhythm phenomenon commonly known as "jet lag," a phenomenon that manifests itself as fatigue. And you don't have to leave home to get it.

The circadian clock is quite literally ticking away in our brain, right down at the "lizard level," and it's been there since we first crawled out of the swamp, regulating all our physiological behavioral functions. In any twenty-four-hour period this clock will regulate our sleep/wake pattern, body temperature, hormones, performance, mood, digestion, and many other human functions.

There it was for thousands of years, happily ticking away, finely tuned, and totally unprepared for Thomas Edison inventing the electric light, transforming us into a twenty-four-hour society in an evolutionary blink of the eye.

Once the circadian clock is moved to a new schedule or time zone, it will begin to adjust, but may take several days to several weeks to physiologically adapt, and we're constantly vulnerable to its effects. Moving from day to night shift and back to days can keep the clock in a continuous state of readjustment, depending on the time between shift changes.

Recent medical research points to another significant phenomenon. The circadian rhythm of body temperature is programmed to have a tidal rhythm, an ebb and flow, with the two daily lowest points between three and five, morning and night. That's when we most feel like sleeping, and when we are most vulnerable.

On August 18, 1993, a Douglas DC8 freighter of American International Airways crashed just short of the runway at Guantanamo Bay, Cuba. The three flight crew sustained serious injuries and the aircraft was destroyed. It was an aviation first when crash investigators laid blame for the crash well and truly at the door of fatigue. There'd been a last-minute decision by an overtired crew to switch to another runway. The flight recorder has the captain saying "just for the heck of it, to see how it is." The first officer responded with an "OK" while the flight engineer said nothing.

And what time did it happen? Four minutes to four in the afternoon, right smack in the middle of the circadian rest point. Looking back to 1959, pilot fatigue resulting in crew error is now being linked to 75 percent of aircraft losses.

When the massive oil tanker *Exxon Valdez* foundered, a media frenzy left the world convinced the accident had been caused by a drunken captain. Ultimately, yes, but in a less direct way. The captain was drunk, but in his bunk. The third mate, who made the error on the bridge, had only had six hours sleep in the previous twenty-four. Investigators are now confident the tragic oil spill was a consequence of fatigue. If the captain being too drunk to operate the ship was the gun, fatigue was the trigger.

The January 28, 1986, *Challenger* accident at Cape Canaveral is now being attributed to decision-makers who stayed awake for long periods to meet deadlines and made the unwise choice to proceed with the mission in the middle of the night.

So how much sleep do we require? Typically people need between six and ten hours. Just two hours less sleep can result in a major decline in alertness and performance—the sleep debt we mentioned before.

How can we tell if someone isn't getting enough sleep? For a start, they exhibit fewer positive emotions and more negative emotions, in other words, they get grumpy. Sleepiness can be held at bay with caffeine, physical activity, and a stimulating environment, such as an interesting conversation. So when people yawn you know they're tired and you're a bore.

Executives who think they can consistently put in twelve- to thirteen-hour days and still be effective are wrong. The quality of their decision-making improves dramatically if they have proper rest. The irony is we appreciate the need for diet and exercise, but we still don't have the same respect for sleep and rest.

> The irony is we appreciate the need for diet and exercise, but we still don't have the same respect for sleep and rest.

We need to see sleep not as wasting valuable work time, but as enabling us to work better and more efficiently. The problem is that people often become work-aholics and avoid sleep as a mask for depression. The busier they are, the less time they have to address the issues they'd rather not face. Believe us, it's always better to face the issues, painful as they may be, rather than burn yourself out with sleep avoidance.

> Sleeping is not wasting valuable work time, but is enabling us to work better and more efficiently.

Get the seven-and-a-half or eight hours' sleep you need and you'll see a difference. Your productivity will increase and your quality of life will increase.

What more excuse do you need? Sleep and stay healthy. And if you're having trouble sleeping, do something about it—talk to your doctor or a sleep specialist. As you reach middle age, there can be physical reasons why your usual sleep patterns are disrupted. Don't let your body "learn" a new pattern of sleeplessness, as it can be hard to break out of—seek advice from the experts to help you get the sleep you need.

And keep your brain active. Otherwise it can lead to depression; you seldom find depression among lively, active people, those with a positive attitude.

"Sharp" is the word for it, sharp of body and mind. That should be your aim. We've already explored the benefits of an active mind, so exercise your brain and it will keep you feeling alive.

There is a tendency for older folk to rely on past experience and not bother too much with the intellectual rigor of youth. Let us warn you very plainly— indulge in lazy thinking at your peril. Use it or lose it applies just as much to your mind as it does to anything else. And keep your sex life in good shape, too. It's good for you, and by far the best thing you can do to improve your skin.

> Keep your sex life in good shape, too. It's good for you, and by far the best thing you can do to improve your skin.

(There you go, what more excuse do you need? And we just saved you a fortune on moisturizers.)

Oh, and stay off drugs, and keep booze consumption to reasonable limits. You don't want to hear this, but you know it's sensible advice, so follow it. Do we really need to mention cigarettes? For many years now cancer researchers have been saying the number one best prevention for cancer is "don't smoke," so if you do; stop.

A survey of the three groups with the highest rate of longevity—the Sardinians, Adventists, and Okinawans— has found that while there are various differences, there are five aspects of life these people all have in common:

- They don't smoke.

- They put family first.

- They are active every day.

- They keep socially engaged.

- They eat fresh fruits and vegetables and whole-grain breads.

What more can we say?

And then there's stress. There's a whole industry devoted to helping you avoid stress. The bad news is that you can't, but the good news is that there's healthy stress as well as unhealthy stress. You just have to learn to separate the two.

You can minimize stress by staying in control. Most stress is associated with a sense of helplessness. You start to feel it's all getting on top of you and, sure enough, it does. It's depressing just thinking about it.

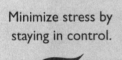

Minimize stress by staying in control.

So stay in control—don't get involved in situations you can't manage. Learn how to walk away and how to actively do nothing. If you leave a space vacant for someone else to fill, you'll often be amazed at the outcome. It's not a case of doing nothing simply because you don't know what to do, instead it's about facing the reality that doing nothing can be a valid and often hugely effective strategy. If you need an impressive historical precedent, Queen

Elizabeth the First, widely regarded as one of the most politically savvy and effective of the British monarchs, based her political strategy on exactly that. Don't react impulsively—do nothing and see what happens. She was famous for it, and had it honed to such a fine degree she drove her opponents nuts.

All successful business people know how to take a loss and walk away, rather than pursuing a lost cause. They've recognized that if they didn't, they'd risk pouring capital—energy and hard cash—down the drain, but there's also the opportunity cost—all those missed chances to do profitable things while they're worrying about trying to fix something that can't be fixed.

> Successful business people know how to take a loss and walk away, rather than pursuing a lost cause.

So it is with life. Something not working out? Move on. This doesn't mean becoming anti-social, because that's another killer. Don't hide away; stay con-nected, mix and mingle. We don't pretend for one moment that it's easy. Some of your friends and family are moving away and, let's be frank, some are moving on, so make new friends. And we're not talking about hanging about with a bunch of boring geriatrics waiting to die while they discuss the good old days. Avoid them like the plague; associate instead

> Don't hide away; stay connected, mix and mingle.

with people who are lively and active and doing interesting things as they look to the future.

Finally there's the issue of a healthy diet, another thriving business with thousands of books on the subject. They all seem to reach pretty much the same conclusion. If you don't eat vegetables, you're more likely to get prostate or breast cancer. Eat too much red meat and you're more likely to get cancer of one sort or another. Eat fatty foods and you're liable for a heart attack or stroke, and food full of sugar will make you fat.

So, moving right along, stick to healthy food. You know what it is. If in doubt, check out the information put out by your local heart foundation.

How much have you spent on your car recently? And your house and garden? How much have you spent on yourself and your own well-being? And how much for pleasure and relaxation? Starting to get the picture? Stay fit and healthy and mentally alert before you lose the option.

Stay fit and healthy and mentally alert before you lose the option.

Key points to remember

✓ Your personal wealth isn't just measured in material assets

✓ Invest as carefully in your physical and mental well-being as you do in the stock exchange

✓ Pay as much attention to your relationships as you do to your other investments

✓ Eat sensibly, sleep, and exercise

✓ Learn to separate good stress and bad stress and know your limits

✓ Learn when to walk away from situations you can't manage

14

I'm off to Cuba

If you're thinking that what we're suggesting is all very well in theory but does it work in the real world, consider the story of our friend Jack.

The Friday lunchtime crowd were engrossed in the fine food and magnificent view across one of the world's most beautiful harbors. David, though, was intent on Jack, his dining companion, one of Sydney's leading commercial lawyers. It had begun harmlessly enough; business completed, they'd switched to the more challenging subject of "what's it all about?"

The lawyer had a dream. Don't we all? When he retired he wanted to go to Cuba. David spent the next fifteen minutes explaining our thoughts on the merits of not retiring; suggesting he remove the word "retirement" from his vocabulary, and asking him what he thought would happen if he did.

The lawyer froze for a few moments, fork poised between mouth and plate. And then the lights went on: one of those wonderful "eureka" moments. It was literally life-changing. For the next half hour Jack waxed lyrical on what this would mean for him. No more planning to live on some deserted beach—if anything, he was going to move closer to the action.

Instead of planning to become an office-bound senior partner, he talked about accumulating a range of new skills for an expanded career path, starting with taking on the more menial jobs he was currently avoiding.

What Jack had worked out, and what made his eyes light up, was that if he was in life for the long haul, then at some stage he'd want to leave the partnership and establish his own private practice. He wanted that practice to provide a "total" service to his clients, so rather than specializing in one narrow aspect of the law, he'd need a significantly expanded range of general skills. He needed to start thinking in terms of retraining and gathering new skills, along with reviving old ones. When Jack left the restaurant he was heading for a travel agent to book a trip to Cuba. He had a whole new view of life and the change was dramatic. "You should spell out your thoughts in a book, and everyone over thirty should read it," he called over his shoulder.

Our lawyer friend, with more than a little help from his own built-in intuitive survival kit, had realized the essence of our message. The entire notion of retirement is a false premise. The good news for the rest of us is that we don't have to be high-flying lawyers to come to terms with life after "retirement" age. All we need to do is take one "R" word out of our vocabulary and replace it with another—Responsibility.

> Take one "R" word out of your vocabulary and replace it with another—Responsibility.

Responsibility is the antidote for retirement. When you assume responsibility for your future, your entire life takes on a new meaning. Now you're in charge, making decisions about the way your life will be lived.

Ask your friends about their future. The moment they mention retirement, don't be surprised to notice how, in that microsecond, their voice takes on a defeatist tone.

They'll stop talking about leading enjoyable, sustainable, and meaningful lives. Please don't let that be you.

> . . . stick to the advice your own heart gives you,
> no one can be truer to you than that;
> since a man's soul often forewarns him better
> than seven watchmen perched on a watch tower.

This is as true today as it was when first written some 2000 years ago in Ecclesiasticus 37—yes, they were writing about intuition way back then. The following words, from the same source, could just as easily have been written today, rather than a few millennia ago. As you read, notice how easy it is to put yourself in the picture.

> Leisure is what gives the scribe the opportunity
> to acquire wisdom;
> the man with few business affairs grows wise.
> How can the ploughman become wise,
> whose sole ambition is to wield the goad;
> driving his oxen, engrossed in their work,
> his conversation is of nothing but cattle?
> His mind is fixed on the furrows he traces,
> and his evenings pass in fattening his heifers.
> So it is with every craftsman and workman,
> Toiling day and night . . .

We can all recognize ourselves here. Working hard day and night—and for what exactly? A straighter furrow, a fatter calf, a happy client, a satisfied boss, promotion, more money, new house, flashier car? You can't fail to be impressed by the perception of the philosopher who penned those words 2000 years ago. Just try inserting any of today's occupations and the same applies. Computer programmers, plumbers, lawyers, carpenters, laborers, or factory workers—everyone so materially and task focused that life slips them by.

Others are starting to break that cycle; it's time for you to do the same. We've already mentioned the Chinese observation, "A journey of a thousand miles begins with the first step." It bears repeating, for right now you should be taking that first step.

— *Step One:* Acknowledge the problem. Once you've done that, half the battle is over.

— *Step Two:* Accept you are never going to retire. You will always be doing something.

— *Step Three:* Do all the things now that you'd planned to do when you retired. Whatever they may be.

Stand back, take a look at what you're doing, where you are, and where you're going or, more to the point, where you're not going. Go to Cuba or Machu Picchu, take up a new sport, or set up a new venture. Follow your dream

> Follow your dream now and it will change your life.

now and it will change your life. Do it now. Leave it until later and there might be precious little left of your life to change.

No one has summed it up better than Steve Jobs, the multi-billionaire force behind Apple computers and the iPod. His is a true rags-to-riches story, a living example of the American dream and, like so many others, he found his road to enlightenment when he had a near-fatal brush with cancer. He shared the resulting wisdom with Stanford University graduates:

Your time is limited, so don't waste it living someone else's life. Don't be trapped by dogma, which is living with the results of other people's thinking. Don't let the noise of others' opinions drown out your inner voice. And most important, have the courage to follow your heart and intuition.

Be a heretic. You have the power to make the choice that is best for you.

Key points
to remember

✓ Responsibility is the antidote to
retirement

✓ Accept that you are never going
to retire, you're always going to be
doing something

✓ Do all the things you've been
planning for retirement NOW

✓ Don't waste the limited time you
have on this Earth by living someone
else's life

15

And don't forget the little car

Brian sells cars. Now, before you begin conjuring up an image of a grinning, pot-bellied, open-armed, congenital liar, complete with greasy hair plastered over a bald spot, bearing down upon you in his white shoes and white tie — Brian is a good guy.

For a start, Brian sells new cars so there is none of the "Only had one careful lady owner, in fact, it's such a bargain I was planning to let my mother have it, but unfortunately she died last week."

No, Brian sells quality, with a cast-iron warranty that guarantees him repeat business from the comfortable suburbs that surround his dealership. His customers are fellow Rotarians. He sells them quality sedans, roadsters to their sons, and station wagons to their wives, and over the years Brian has become a great observer of human nature.

He understands how important it is to his aspiring customers to be seen in the "right" car, and for their wives and children to be seen in the "right" car. They judge others by the cars they drive and fully expect to be judged accordingly themselves. Brian, businessman that he is, knows how to exploit this. He would never, for example, point out that the truly wealthy buy modest reliability and expect it to last forever. The conversation changes dramatically when it comes to the last car.

He sees them coming from a long way off. Heads bowed, shoulders slumped, they hover around the edge of the showroom. Once, they would have strode purposefully to the gleaming new convertible for a brief daydream, thinking "How would I look in that!," before giving serious attention to the latest, fully-optioned executive chariot.

Now, they potter around the back of the showroom where the smaller, budget cars are, asking lots of questions—baggage capacity, fuel economy, length of warranty. And, most importantly of all: how long will it last? Brian watches as they do the mental calculations. One question, always unspoken, is paramount. "Will it last me out?"

Brian probably thinks an existentialist is something that belongs in a gearbox, but in his own way, he is every bit a philosopher and a great judge of human nature. He understands the "last car" syndrome all too well.

There comes a point in everyone's life when they accept their own mortality. Inevitably they ask, "What's the point?" The point, as the more thoughtful have concluded, is to be, and keep on being, taking responsibility for your own life. The sad alternative is to retreat into a meaningless world of nothingness, a slow form of suicide. And nothing, absolutely nothing, sums it up better than the "last car" syndrome. The last "little" car.

Brian sees and hears it all too often, "Well, I'm getting on a bit now and need a car to see me out. Something for pottering about in, not too expensive, not too heavy on the gas." What they're really saying is that they're waiting to die, entering into a form of voluntary home detention. When you think that your "retirement" could last for thirty years, doesn't that seem a bit extreme? Thirty years of low mileage — if that isn't being half-dead, what is?

This is a great trap you must not fall into, under any circumstances. The little car that will "see us out," together with the new little home next door to all the other poor souls "waiting for God." Now you can all hold meetings to discuss that all-consuming crack in the footpath.

And for goodness sake don't go anywhere in the new little car in case you wear it out too fast. Before you know it, the new little car has become a mobile coffin and every time you use it you'll be worrying about whether it's going to "see you out." You're actually hoping to conk out before your car? Sound scary?

> Before you know it, the new little car has become a mobile coffin.

Can you believe people actually do this to themselves? Well, they do. Please, don't let it be you.

And why do we so willingly change from being alive and vibrant to deadly dull? Because we've been conned into accepting the cycle — live, work, retire, die. Notice

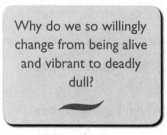

Why do we so willingly change from being alive and vibrant to deadly dull?

the only time we're allowed to live is at the beginning? Then it's all downhill from there. Years of work, retirement, and death.

What if the cycle was a line of "living" that included working? Sure, death is the final inevitability, but how can you live if you're only focused on the end? And who says we have to prepare for it gradually, over a lifetime soured and diminished by worry?

What would happen if you didn't get the "little car"? First of all you'd stay upright. No more droopy shoulders. No more terminal worry. No more silly notions of shrinking yourself into that mobile coffin or tiny home while you await the Grim Reaper's knock. His first words are likely to be, "You called?"

You buy a little car to see you out at your peril, because that will be the moment you give up. Don't get us wrong. We have nothing against small, economical cars and we're not for a moment suggesting you go out and buy some ozone-destroying gas-guzzler. Far from it. Just don't, whatever you do, think in terms of a little car *to see you out*.

To avoid the "last little car" syndrome, conquer the fear of growing old.

To avoid the "last little car" syndrome, you'll have to conquer the fear we have of growing old, which encompasses the fear that we won't have enough money, and we'll be alone. And nowhere is this better illustrated than in China.

There was a time when we looked to China as a model example of how to deal with an ageing society. It was simple. The old lived with their children. Not any more. Now the Chinese are having to deal with the previously Western phenomenon of the empty nest, where parents live alone in their old age. In a land where this was unheard of, close to 40 percent of Shanghai's elderly now live apart from their children. This has led to a sense of betrayal that worsens when either partner dies. All the evidence shows surviving partners are highly likely to become sick and depressed for the simple reason they live alone.

As a consequence, these lonely, depressed, old people are volunteering to do something that previously would have brought great shame. They're lining up to enter old folks' homes, knowing full well they're sending a signal that their children have deserted them, but even the shame is preferable to living alone.

They manage to justify this with talk of not wanting to be a burden on their successful offspring and, thanks to China's one-child policy, it's usually just the one.

The fear is everywhere. It's not just a fear of loneliness — it's about feeling safe too. Old people are worried, prisoners in their own homes, for fear of becoming a victim of crime. For the record, statistics show that people over the age of sixty are three times less likely to be affected by crime than younger citizens, but still they worry. They worry about their health, they worry their kids will put them in an old folks' home and sell the house, they worry about paying their rent . . . . Endless worry.

Reflect for a moment on the words of Sir Winston Churchill, "When I look back on all the worries, I remember the story of the old man who said on his deathbed that he had a lot of trouble in his life, most of which never happened."

> 'I remember the story of the old man who said on his deathbed that he had a lot of trouble in his life, most of which never happened.'
>
> Sir Winston Churchill

Can you imagine the great man peering in the window of a car dealership, admiring the smallest model and pondering the "low-cost, no-hassle ownership" experience on offer? He would no doubt have been captivated by its compact size, making it ideal for easy parking at the shopping center. Should he have ventured into the showroom, the renowned orator would have been captured by a sales spiel that drew his attention to such "senior-friendly features" as the adjustable driver's seat and tilt-and-telescopic steering wheel.

Listening to the combination of compact size and fuel economy, not to mention price, Sir Winston would have drawn heavily on his cigar as the salesman proffered his trump card, "Sir may care to know that Green seniors are most attracted to the Retiree Hybrid, which boasts ultra-low emissions."

No disrespect to the little cars, but you may now share our vision of the man, who became prime minister of

Britain for the second time at the age of seventy-seven, stomping off down the street in a cloud of smoke, in search of something a tad more exciting.

That said, let us repeat, we're not against little cars, or saving fuel or getting something which is easier to park—these are all thoroughly legitimate reasons for buying a smaller car. We're just against it being the "final" little car. If you do buy one, or you already have one, don't see it as being your last. It's just a car.

So get a life, make some lifestyle changes for the better, and start by looking at change as positive, not negative. Have new experiences that will create new pathways in your brain to let your mind know you're still alive.

> So get a life, make some lifestyle changes for the better, and start by looking at change as positive, not negative.

The trick is to turn that old saying about "all work and no play makes Jack a dull boy" on its head. Think about it for a moment. Work is what keeps you going, gives life purpose and meaning, while play is the deserved treat, the rewarding part of a fulfilling and continuing life. All play and no work would soon make Jack a very dull boy indeed.

We've been convinced to work hard for forty years with the promise of then being able to do nothing for whatever time we may have left—and as we feel obliged to constantly remind you, that could be thirty or more years. This results in the bizarre notion that, rather than having a naturally balanced existence, in which work, play, and relaxation are given equal priority throughout our entire life, they have to be somehow compartmentalized, divided up according to our age.

We refused to buy into it when we were younger—as children we set about packing in as much as possible, as though there was no tomorrow. We behaved as though every day was our last. We wanted it all, and we got it, or as much as we could.

As we grew into teenagers and into our twenties, did we suddenly start to think about what tomorrow might hold? Yes, of course, and we began to plan our careers. We chose partners with whom to have children and share a life. We made mistakes that we shrugged off and got on with the rest of our lives. Did we constantly worry? Of course not.

Not that we were entirely stupid. We had a sense of our own mortality, but the secret was not to constantly worry about it. Whatever would be, would be.

Then we woke up one fine morning, ready to face another day, to be confronted by an article or television news item about baby boomers reaching retirement age. We were, and indeed are, expected to react with a collective "Uh oh, that's me! I have to stop now and retire."

There is suddenly this expectation that we'll all step off life's escalator and into one of those French art-house movies where the dialogue, plot, characters, and even the set have no meaning. Reality replaced by a metaphysical world. That's all very well in the cinema and the wine bar afterwards, where we might sit around discussing the nature of knowledge and existence—in other words, showing off.

We're not here to live in an unreal world, and can there truly be anything more unreal than this retirement business? So get back on the escalator and start looking ahead to a life of active participation in both work and play. Get off the sideline and back on the field of play, where you belong.

There's a brilliant advertising campaign based on the ideas we've been talking about, with the catch phrase "When was the last time you did something for the first time?" It shows the delight on the face of a Japanese grandmother swooping off the helipad of the amazing sail-shaped hotel in Dubai, and two Africans giggling and trying not to look uncool as they speed past their hotel receptionist and into the street where it's snowing.

We're not suggesting you can afford to do it in quite that style, but the principle is the same—have new experiences and get back your childhood sense of delight and excitement, regardless of your age. It's still there by the way, no matter how well you may have buried it, so start digging.

Henry Ford—who produced the iconic Model T Ford, which sold in the millions and ran forever—had a truly simple philosophy for life:

> **If you think you can do a thing, or
> think you can't do a thing, you're right.**

Smart fellow.

Without wishing to sound like some of those motivational types, get your life back and rediscover your vitality. Seriously, we're not suggesting a totally selfish and irresponsible approach to life, far from it. We're merely suggesting you take back control of your own life and refuse point-blank to allow the system to pigeon-hole you as a lost cause.

Of course you must look ahead; we all need to plan. But plan for an active life with a purpose other than merely existing. The trick here, and we make no apology for repeating ourselves, is to plan for an ongoing life, not retirement.

For your own peace of mind, for your own sanity, be bold and spend the rest of your life making things happen, rather than waiting for them to happen to you. Bring back the passion and the positive approach that should have driven you for so much of your life. And if it hasn't, then make sure you don't waste any more time—you deserve an exciting and interesting and fulfilling life. And, while on the subject of being positive, remember to stay away from the negative people—their negativity is depressing and infectious. It's the easiest thing in the world to sit around feeling sorry for yourself. Taking back control and seizing opportunities may be harder, but it's a heck of a lot more rewarding.

> Stay away from the negative people—their negativity is depressing and infectious.

When John Calvin, whose thinking dominates so much of Western culture, was asked what he would do if he thought the world was going to end the next day he said: "If I was certain the world was going to end tomorrow I'd go out and plant an apple tree. Because it is only by hope that we live."

So as soon as you've deleted the "R" virus, go out and plant your apple tree. You'll find the world is alive and well and awaiting your return. It needs lively souls to nourish it, not dull ones to drain it. People who are getting on with their lives don't have to think about getting a small car to see them out. They get the car that suits their lifestyle, confident that when that lifestyle changes, for whatever reason, they'll get another car to suit. But it'll never be a car to see them out. Never.

Key points to remember

✓ The little car to see you out is nothing more than a mobile coffin—avoid it at all costs

✓ New experiences let your mind know you're still alive

✓ Who says work, play and relaxation have to be compartmentalized according to our age?

✓ Refuse to be pigeon-holed by the date on your birth certificate

16

Go where the action is

The next biggest mistake for self-imposed retirees, after buying the little car, is to move to the beach, the country, a distant suburb, small town, or retirement village. They want to "get away from it all."

What they don't realize is that we should only "get away" when we're stressed. As our stress levels drop, we need to be back in the middle of it, where the action is, where there's some life, where no one cares about the crack in the footpath. Plan for pleasure and excitement and be a vital part of it, where everything you could possibly require is right there on your doorstep.

Unless it's absolutely necessary, avoid the retirement home where your children will come to visit you twice a year: once at Christmas and then again on their birthday—*their* birthday note, not yours. Better still, don't move at all.

The real-estate sign outside a house in a quiet street said it all: *Moving On*. Why? Where were they going? It was an easy walk to all the amenities in a great community. We just had to ask.

Roger and Margaret were a classic example of everything we've been talking about. Their family had left home and the house was now too big, involving too much maintenance. They were selling to buy a smaller house somewhere quieter, in a village. That sounds nice. A retirement village. Oh, dear.

> The retirement village, no matter how well it's dressed up, is still an institution.

The retirement village, no matter how well it's dressed up, is still an institution. We need look no further than the definition of an institution to make us more than a little wary: *an organized pattern of group behavior, established and generally accepted as a fundamental part of a culture.* Oh really? So was slavery.

And if that doesn't deter you from the prospect, again we refer you to the definition of what lies ahead should you become institutionalized: *apathetic and dependent after long term residence in an institution.*

So why do people head for the institution, the retirement village?

Because they think they have a cunning plan—to sell the family home, make a tidy profit, save on maintenance, have the freedom to travel, and, as needs dictate, move up through the village structure to a studio apartment and possibly even a hospital bed. In short: safety and security is their dream. That's the plan. Let's examine it in detail.

Once you've sold the house, finding the retirement village is reasonably straightforward, they're springing up everywhere. And having bought your little box, there should be plenty left for a cruise before settling into life in the retirement village. That's when you discover institutions have rules for everything.

Now, that might very well suit you, but as Roger and Margaret thought about it they could see themselves peacefully and unobtrusively withering on the vine as they obeyed all those rules.

The *Moving On* sign came down. The retirement village was forgotten. They would stay where they were. Yes, their home might have a room or two more than they needed, but that extra space would be needed later when grandchildren came to visit. They were going to stay in their own community, where all their friends were.

Robert and Mary had a very successful business, and in their mid-fifties decided to fulfil a lifelong dream of retiring to the country. They were so certain this was their ideal future they sold their city home and made the move permanent.

The first month was everything they'd dreamed off, a wonderful merry-go-round of sleep, golf, swimming, tennis, and more glorious sleep. The second month was almost as rewarding, but by the end of the third month the novelty was beginning to wear off. One moment they had successful careers and the next they were staring into space, admiring the view.

Thankfully, they were smart enough to spot the danger before it overwhelmed them. They bought into a small furniture-making business they then helped turn around and expand. It's now the largest employer in the district and exports worldwide.

Even today they can hardly believe how close they came to the retirement nightmare. Robert and Mary were still running the business and driving export expansion when they turned seventy-five. No more self-administered euthanasia for them, they've had a lucky escape and are infinitely happier for it.

Please don't misunderstand us, there's nothing wrong with retirement centers for people with no other options. Indeed, they fulfil a vital role in the community, but they shouldn't be an automatic selection for everyone, which is the way far too many people see them. That includes people old before their time—and their long-suffering relatives, who often see the retirement village as a welcome relief. At last, somewhere to put those troublesome relatives.

And it's all too easy to rationalize; Aunt Mabel will be so much safer there, no danger of her wandering out into the road. What if she causes an accident and kills someone? Brilliant—something that will probably never happen is being used as an excuse to put a healthy, vibrant woman into an institution. Our message to the Aunt Mabels of this world is to hang onto your lives, and only make such a drastic move if and when you have to.

Staying where you are, where the action is, involves recognizing the difference between action and passive acquiescence. Action is about involvement, the absolute opposite of being passive. Trust us, being passive is a death knell, rather like accepting anything and everything that happens without putting up any resistance. And where does the word come from? The Latin word *passivus*, which means, quite appropriately, "susceptible to suffering."

We'll say it yet again; Get your life back and enjoy it, or suffer

> Get your life back and enjoy it, or suffer the self-inflicted consequences.

the self-inflicted consequences. We say self-inflicted because we all have choices. Letting go of being active and becoming passive has severe consequences, but it is something people *choose* to do. Don't make that mistake.

Everything we say in this book is geared to encouraging you towards *active* resistance, to connect with your inner survival mechanisms and go for it! Stay where the action is, where life goes on. Stay where there are teenagers behaving like teenagers, and lawnmowers and noisy parties—in other words, where there are people getting on with life. Life as it's always been, so wonderfully unpredictable, diverse, dysfunctional and even irritating. This is the environment where you've lived and survived all your life. Don't opt out now, no matter what anyone tells you. You can find your own action, right where you are.

> Stay where the action is, where life goes on.

You can always buy yourself a long white limo—that's what Wayne did.

We won't embarrass Wayne, an accomplished and experienced marine engineer, by listing all the innovations he's been personally responsible for. Suffice to say, if you've ever traveled very fast in a small boat, you can probably thank Wayne for some part of the experience.

However, as is often the case, inventors don't always receive their just rewards, especially when they work for companies that put shareholders first. That was Wayne's lot in life, not that you'll ever hear him complain. His real satisfaction came from seeing his ideas put into motion. When he was shown the door on the allotted day, he had enough put aside for a "comfortable" retirement. But what would he do?

He started a book. He organized the garden. He went on a world trip. What next? What Wayne did was to buy the longest, whitest stretch limo you've ever seen. It wasn't new and it certainly didn't cost an arm and a leg, but did it look the part! There was a cocktail cabinet, a full entertainment system and enough room to seat a football team. Wayne can be found outside the swankiest hotels, collecting visitors for fully guided tours of his city and the surrounding countryside.

The phone never stops ringing from people wanting Wayne for their wedding or that special night out. Note: it's Wayne they want—sure, the limo makes a bit of a statement, but it's Wayne who adds the real value.

A lifetime of experience, dealing with everyone from the shop floor to the boardroom, prepared him to cope with anything the back seat of his limo could throw at him. And it got him thinking. If he could do it, what about all those other business people in retirement limbo?

There's now a fleet of limos—granted they're somewhat shorter and more discreet than the first—and a team of drivers, each and every one of them in their "retirement" years. At first, young executives found it uncomfortable being driven about by men and women they recognized as former corporate high-flyers. Not any more, they don't. Wayne's Cabbies have not only established a stunningly successful business, charging a healthy margin for their corporate services, but many of the drivers have become de facto mentors to some of their more discerning regulars.

Key points to remember

✔ We only need to get away when we're stressed—we don't need to stay away

✔ Life going on around you can be noisy, crazy, and sometimes irritating, but it's also stimulating, so don't run away from it

✔ The more action there is around you, the more options you have

17

May you rest in peace

Retirement village or, worse still, rest home. The names say it all. We have been constantly amazed, when visiting retirement villages, to meet so few vibrant and healthy people, with fewer still actively working and making a valuable contribution. We've also noticed a considerable difference in villages that described themselves as "lifestyle" rather than "retirement." The lifestyle villages have a much greater range of active people who were still employed, some even full-time.

We were surprised by the effect that the name "retirement village" seemed to have. Imagine for a moment that Oak View Retirement Village became Oak View Village. Rather than Millside Retirement Village, what if it was Millside Village? Now, where would you rather live? And how might your approach to life differ, depending on whether you lived in a retirement village or a village?

Have you ever seen the retirement shuffle? Take a walk past an old folks' home and watch them shuffle. This often has little to do with the fact they can no longer stand upright and stride about, with obvious exceptions for those with physical disabilities—for some residents it's all about having nowhere to go, and taking as long as humanly possible about getting there.

> Think about sitting in that self-same chair with nothing planned for the next few hours or days or weeks or years.

As you read this book, it's all too easy to dismiss the thought that this is ever going to happen to you. Think again. Think about sitting in that self-same chair with nothing planned for the next few hours or days or weeks or years. If that doesn't make you feel depressed, we should really think about giving you your money back, as you're clearly beyond help.

> Now visualize yourself living in the wider community, continuing to work either full-time or part-time and getting on with enjoying your life.

Now visualize yourself living in the wider community, continuing to work either full-time or part-time and getting on with enjoying your life. Were we imagining that or did we just see your shoulders lift?

As we've mentioned before, the majority of boomers think they'll be able to sell their homes, buy a smaller one and live off the profit. There was brief mention earlier that the housing bubble will burst. It has to. The tens of millions of people who right now are banking on their home paying for their retirement could be left staring ruin and hardship in the face.

In the latter years of the last century and early this century, there's been a worldwide surge in the cost of housing in the developed world, with house prices soaring by a staggering 50 percent. And, as light follows day, the developers swooped, leading to a massive construction boom.

Billions were invested and homeowners everywhere celebrated their good luck with a visit to the car dealership and the appliance shop and the travel center, spending like there was no tomorrow. Why not? They were rich. Look at how much their houses were worth!

The world's economy wasn't being driven by innovation, expansion, productivity, entrepreneurs, or imaginative governments. It was being driven by rising house prices and debt. It has been, and still is, a banker's bonanza.

Why has this been happening? Well, there are no glaringly obvious reasons. Parts of Europe and Australasia had significant waves of political and economic immigrants fleeing repression or poverty in their own country to pursue a better lifestyle. With some exceptions, the majority were usually poor people chasing poorly paid jobs.

Inflation wasn't going through the roof, nor were wages or rents. It came down to speculation, and as history has taught us time and again, when too many people climb aboard the speculative bandwagon the bubble bursts. Always. And, as always, this will lead to heartache as people pay off mortgages on homes worth less than they paid for them.

Millions of property-rich baby boomers who are assuming that they'll be able to sell their home, buy a cheaper one and live off the profit are about to be kicked where it hurts most. Their dream of buying into a retirement village, with hundreds of thousands in the bank, is going to be just that—a dream.

In Australia, for example, the majority of households are already either single occupant or single-parent families. Who'll be buying the large family homes today's boomers want to sell? The large family is gradually dying out and becoming a thing of the past.

Rising house prices make people feel wealthy, but it's an illusion. Mind you, the banks don't think so—they happily lend more and more money on the rising value of residential homes. People are borrowing to pay today's bills in the hope of solving all their problems with a quick and lucrative sale tomorrow.

> Rising house prices make people feel wealthy, but it's an illusion.

The reality is, all those other baby boomers will be trying to sell their homes at the same time and, more to the point, trying to sell them to a generation with a whole new outlook on marriage, children, and home ownership.

So who *are* going to buy all those big, roomy family homes? It won't be the poor immigrants imported to fill the jobs of a retiring workforce, and we can't rely on our children's children, as they're showing signs of being opposed to the very notion of having any offspring.

And it's not as if housing slumps on a massive scale haven't happened before—look at the United States in the 1930s, the United Kingdom in the 1980s, and Japan in the 1990s.

But if you want to see a truly crazy property market, look no further than Ireland, Dublin in particular. House prices are rising by an annual rate of 29 percent, off the back of rises in excess of 100 percent during the late 1990s. Things got so frantic banks began lending on the basis of a buyer's potential future earnings and parental guarantees.

The Irish economy, growing by leaps and bounds with a per capita income outstripping that of Britain, has set such a frenetic pace of growth it's been labelled the Celtic Tiger. Immigration has boomed along with the economy, as the Irish began returning home, rather than queuing up to leave.

In situations like this, what tends to happen is that the central banks step in to dampen the housing market by forcing up interest rates to keep inflation down. If not, the basic rules of supply and demand come to the fore and force prices down. Now think about your friends and neighbors and the eye-watering mortgages they've taken on to pay for their slice of suburban heaven.

Before the British housing market collapse in the 1980s that left many people with mortgages larger than the value of their home, there was a standard real-estate joke. The salesman would show a couple around a house and then remark "Of course, if you would like to see a more expensive one, I could always show you this one again tomorrow."

It's no laughing matter when the bubble bursts around your ears. And there's a very real chance the current property boom could go bang with the same sonic proportions as the dotcom bust of the late nineties, although with far greater consequences. While not everyone had a dotcom share, practically everyone has a house and, for reasons that defy logic, speculating in housing has become an international trend on a par with owning an iPod.

> The current property boom could go bang with the same sonic proportions as the dotcom bust of the late nineties.

The good news is that all of this is irrelevant, unless you've borrowed to the hilt against the artificially inflated value of your home, or are banking on selling it to finance your retirement. And if you now have no intention of retiring, it doesn't matter. You can carry on living in your home and get on with the rest of your life. You can ignore all those ads urging you to scale down, suggesting you sell your house and hand the profit over to some young financial genius who'll invest it for you and protect your future.

You're not going to live in a retirement village, but you might if they took out the word "retirement" and made it a worthwhile "lifestyle" experience. If they had tennis courts, not bowling greens, and Internet cafés instead of tea trolleys. You're going to carry on living in the real world with a real life.

What we're talking about here is fundamental. It has nothing to do with why you might get up in the morning and everything to do with the fact you have a free will. And while we stress that you should avoid the retirement village trap, we're not by any means advocating you don't change. Change by all means, just don't retire. Next time there's an international gathering of world leaders, take a close look at them. Notice how politicians refuse to retire? They hang on in there for one more election, one more term. And no matter where you live, you'll be able to think of a leader who hung on in there too long. Men and women, once respected for their vision, daring, and determination to make a difference, who eventually paid the ultimate price of public humiliation at the ballot box. That's one of the reasons we have democratic elections—to get rid of people who've been there too long, and have come to believe they're born to rule rather than serve.

And all too often that's what people facing retirement are afraid of, the humiliation of staying on beyond their welcome, and being unceremoniously shown the door. But unless you're a power-hungry politician this has nothing to do with you. As we've seen, there is growing recognition of the valuable and continuing role people can play in their later years.

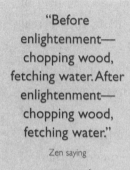

"Before enlightenment—chopping wood, fetching water. After enlightenment—chopping wood, fetching water."

Zen saying

There is a Zen saying: "Before enlightenment—chopping wood, fetching water. After enlightenment—chopping wood, fetching water." When you know what you're doing, there doesn't need to be any drastic change.

A headline from a Los Angeles newspaper summed it up beautifully—"Legend Arthur Winston, 100, Dies After Brief Retirement." Were they writing about some famous sportsman, businessman, lawyer, or politician? No. Arthur Winston cleaned Los Angeles buses and trains, missing just one day in seventy-two years of work, the day his wife died. Arthur retired the day after he turned 100. This was someone who described himself as nothing more than a "working man" who strongly believed a person should stay active as long as possible.

"Keep working. Work and work some more."

"Stop in one place too long, you freeze up," the paper quoted him as saying. "Freeze up, you're done for . . . Keep working. Work and work some more."

Now, we can't all be legends like Arthur Winston, but we can keep going with dignity. There's a degree of irony in the coverage of his story. Arthur was a hero because he lived to be 100, the fact he worked for so long was reported with glee and everyone shared the moment.

Yet the vast majority of stories about people working into their late sixties and seventies are accompanied by tales of woe. These people are often portrayed as victims, working because they have to, because they didn't plan properly for their retirement. The idea of people working on because they *want* to totally escapes most journalists. Most young journalists.

Do the Rolling Stones still tour the world and excite legions of fans because they need the money? Of course not. These granddaddies of rock are up there on the stage, the most exciting rock 'n' roll band in the world, because they love it. Sure, they now go home to their wives, children, and grandchildren, but they love what they do. They're motivated and have a reason to get up in the morning. They're engaged with the rest of the world. Retire? Where's the satisfaction in that?

That's why we should all ecstatically greet the news that more and more employers are looking to keep their existing workers on, accepting that it makes far more sense to make an allowance for age, rather than having to hire and then train youngsters, if indeed you can find them. That's also why we welcome the new thinking that it makes sense to encourage people to put off retirement, on the promise of an even bigger pension if they do.

We're not naïve, we realize the underlying hope is that these people will die working and not actually collect their pensions, but that misses the point. It's the retirement that kills them, not the work.

We've visited lifestyle villages where people have sports cars in the garage and run successful businesses from their homes, and we applaud them. They are the exception rather than the rule, though, as we've also come across retirement establishments that have a problem with pets, let alone visiting grandchildren.

The point is that moving into such a community sends the signal that you've also given up the ghost. The answer is to stay in the real world. Put retirement out of sight and out of mind.

Key points to remember

✓ Don't put all your financial eggs in the "sell my house" basket

✓ Make being mortgage-free a priority

✓ When you know what you're doing, change doesn't have to be drastic to be effective

✓ Freeze up and you're done for . . . Robert Winston, 100 years old

18

Live at the Hilton

Sound silly? Not really.

For twelve years, Arnold virtually lived at the Hilton; business was brisk and the hotel became his home away from home. On arrival, he was always greeted with a "welcome home." For Arnold, it was a business address when away from his base, but it soon became far more than that.

Arnold and Sue are an enlightened couple who've worked out that life is about living, not dying. Arnold is a well-traveled businessman, with Sue as his minder, personal assistant, and wife. Together they make a great team with a mutual interest in travel, so at a time when most people would be giving up and retiring, they decided to combine their occupation with their passion. While retirement wasn't on their radar screens, living was. They didn't give up work, instead they gave up their office and their home.

They chose to spend their time traveling and negotiated a terrific rate with the Hilton chain. They moved in and became full-time residents of one of the world's great hotels. They were now free to work through their retirement years, traveling where they pleased and always staying at the Hilton.

Everything they needed was at their fingertips. Freedom to work, travel and explore, enjoy each other's company, and do the things that gave them real pleasure. They were spending their time doing what they wanted to do, while also working and enjoying life.

Note those words "spending their time." Time was an asset they had invested in and accumulated as part of their "wealth." One of the additional assets they now had time to enjoy was time itself.

Sound silly? Just look at what Arnold and Sue saved on—run your finger down the list and add it up for yourself.

Rent

Maintenance

House insurance

Homeowner's insurance

Furniture

Parking

Common charges

Power

Heating

Telephone/Fax/Internet

Pool maintenance

Cleaning

Gardening

Gym membership

Security

In addition to these significant savings, they enjoyed other benefits from living at the Hilton.

A great address

Terrific surroundings in which to entertain their friends, family, clients, and business associates

A dream lifestyle

On-site gymnasium

Heated swimming and spa pool

Always in the heart of lively and cosmopolitan cities

Throw in the tax-deductible business savings, and what more could you ask for? The idea of moving into a hotel might sound strange—after all, it flies in the face of everything we've been brought up to aspire to: owning our own home. We've been convinced this is important because it panders to our basic primal need for safety.

Most people associate home with a feeling of security, but that has more to do with being with their family than the physical safety of the home itself. The flip side of this rationale is that adult children are able to justify putting their aged parents into a "home" for their own "safety."

Safety and fear are two sides of the same coin. We're programmed to seek safety and survival with a built-in avoidance of danger. In times of great stress we get an automatic adrenalin injection to our system, which instantly activates our bodies into what's commonly called a fight or flight response. Do we fight, become aggressors and attack? Do we run to avoid a danger that's too great for us to confront? Either way, the objective is to ensure our safety and survival.

We're afraid of "home invasion" even though the likelihood of it happening to us is practically nil, while the fear of being poor and alone in retirement is one of the greatest fears we all share.

Arnold and Sue are happy and contented because they've achieved safety in bucketfuls by living at the Hilton. Not much chance of a home invasion there. We should learn from them, and then take our own *intuitive* advice about getting the best out of our own lives. Remember: this is your real life, not a rehearsal.

> This is your real life, not a rehearsal.
>
>

Having doubts about your future is the first clear message that something is wrong. Doubt is your right brain saying "I don't think so." So listen to yourself. No one knows better what's best for you.

Hadyn is now an enlightened follower of this theory. An architect, he was heading for burnout. This was a man who essentially was at the top of his game, with everything going for him. The fact he'd designed a home was a major selling point that real-estate agents took every opportunity to feature in their advertisements. The finest young graduates queued up to work for his firm. He had more business than he could handle, and a wife, children, and home straight out of a women's magazine. He had it all.

Or so it seemed. Behind the façade Hadyn was miserable. Everyone kept telling him how successful and lucky he was, then asking when he planned to retire. He was facing extreme pressure to do something that was totally against his better nature.

Facing the expectation of retirement, he thought there was something wrong with him because he really didn't want to retire. We know this sounds bizarre, but it's increasingly common for people to feel personally driven to continue working yet made to feel guilty for thinking such radical thoughts.

We took him aside, gave him our thoughts—this book in a nutshell—and he saw the light. He now takes every Wednesday off to relax. This achieves two purposes. It keeps his associates happy because they see him slowing down, satisfying their need for him to work his way into retirement, just as they plan to do one day. As for Hadyn, he uses the "day off" to catch up on reading, and finds he's become much more productive in the four days he does work now he's less stressed. Because, just as it's important to get adequate sleep, it's also crucial to take regular breaks.

Hadyn is now what the psychologists would call "congruent" or, in plain English, he's got it all together. He's already worked five years past the time when people traditionally retire, and this septuagenarian has no intention of stopping.

You don't have to call the Hilton. Just get in the driving seat of your own life journey.

Key points to remember

✓ Think outside the square of owning your own four walls

✓ Time is an important asset—spend it wisely

✓ Taking regular breaks is crucial to your physical and emotional well-being

✓ Listen to your intuition—no one else knows what's better for you

19

What huskies know

When huskies are young and keen, they pull at 110 percent. Then, as their energy and desire to pull lessens, they decrease their workload to the point of walking beside the sledge, or even behind it, giving the younger dogs encouragement. The one thing they never do is sit on the sledge.

So why on earth would an elderly human, who can probably still pull at 70 percent of their peak capacity, suddenly stop, climb up on the sledge, and expect the younger generation to pull them along?

This complaint is being heard around the world, loud and clear, and often loudest from the bureaucrats. A CEO of a major hospital complained recently about the cost of services to the elderly, "Sure the elderly may have paid taxes all their lives, but the reality is they used to think that if they slipped and fell we'd give them a walking stick. Now they all want a hip replacement and we just can't afford them!"

This sensitive soul went on to point out that a quarter of all operations, a third in some countries, were performed on people in the last year of their lives. This all added up, so the argument went, to a huge waste of resources. Unfortunately this point of view is gaining currency throughout the world. Yes, you paid your taxes, but that money's all been spent. Most of it, we might add, on the wages of the same bureaucrats who now argue the futility of repairing old bodies.

What this does is reinforce everything we've been saying. Be a huskie and keep going, depend on no one. Look after yourself, and under no circumstances rely on being rescued from the bottom of the cliff. And don't grumble about it—you're only old when *you* decide, so don't let anyone else decide for you.

It's still all too easy to fall into the trap of "growing old" and surrounding yourself with moaners and whiners endlessly carrying on about their aching bones, varicose veins, and sagging arms.

Quite often they're forty-year-olds, sad sacks who are old before their time. By the time they get into their fifties they start complaining about the state of the nation's youth and how disgusting it is that they're taking drugs and having sex. Excuse us, but where were these people in the sixties and seventies? They certainly can't have been living on the same planet as us. These are the people who try to reinvent their youth by going to a Rolling Stones concert and then complain about the size of the crowd, and all the pushing and shoving.

If our friends complain about aching bones it's because they've just finished a marathon or cross-country cycle race. They certainly don't harp on about how old they are, they leave that to the boring fifty-year-old loser back in the office, waiting to retire.

> If our friends complain about aching bones it's because they've just finished a marathon or cross-country cycle race.

And here's the rub. To successfully beat the retirement blues you must never think of getting up on the sledge. Constantly remind yourself—think young, stay young.

> Constantly remind yourself—think young, stay young.

British actor Sir Michael Caine is in his seventies and still working. When interviewed by the BBC, he summed up the retirement notion rather succinctly with, "You don't retire from this business, the business retires you." He has no intention of letting go, believing he has years of active film-making left—and if show business does retire him, he'll find another business.

In short, stop talking about getting old and stop looking at the sledge. Don't make age and illness your currency, because no one really wants to know about all your grumbles. When you wax on about your age and your illnesses

> Don't make age and illness your currency, because no one really wants to know about all your grumbles.

the other person is probably thinking, "How can I escape from this morbid, depressing, and boring person?"

One of the great myths is the inability of people to bridge the age gap. Young people can and do enjoy talking to older people. Most youngsters, the twenty- and thirty-somethings, are smart enough to know that while they think they know everything, the oldies generally know more than them. It only goes wrong when the oldie trots out one of those infamous lines, "I remember when" or "Wait 'til you're my age."

If you have an old view on life, then you're old. Or as the ageless film star Joan Collins likes to put it, "You may not like getting older, but it's better than the alternative."

> Baby boomers are getting heartily sick and tired of being told they're old and will have to retire soon.

Thankfully, there is hope, as more and more baby boomers are getting heartily sick and tired of being told they're old and will have to retire soon. Some of them are putting up a fight and their positive attitude is beginning to catch on. They're opting to start their own companies, and already there are enough of them doing this for some measurable facts to start coming in.

Worldwide the majority of new companies fail, yet in Wales they're singing a very different tune with one of the highest rates of business start-ups among the over-fifties. A massive 85 percent of those companies thrive and succeed. Companies started by enterprising, lively people who refuse point-blank to fall into the "retire at sixty-five" trap their parents fell into. They're refusing to get up on the sledge.

The great mind-switch these people have made is to keep working, not because they have to but because they want to—after all, it's what they do. Their jobs and their professions are a manifestation of their skill and their personalities. Work is who they are and a reflection of their existence, not something they do just to put food on the table. And they refuse to be put in boxes.

We have the dreadful label of "baby boomer" and yet we vary in age by as much as nearly twenty years and come from all walks of life. Some of us are richer than others, better educated and in better health. And we certainly don't all vote the same way. Some of us can actually program a video or DVD recorder. Well, alright, not that many of us. But we can use computers and mobile phones and we can keep working and living joy-filled lives.

The general acceptance that people should retire is packed with ironies. Notice how popes are allowed to keep going till they drop, even when it might be obvious to mere mortals that they're a tad over-the-hill. Notice how judges, the people who determine right and wrong and interpret the laws of the land, can be found sitting in the world's most esteemed courts well into their eighties, in some cases until they die.

One of the world's great appliance manufacturers makes a point of keeping its founding engineers on the payroll.

They have a desk in the engineering department, they come and go as they please, and are valued for their institutional knowledge and all-round wisdom. And whenever a major problem arises, they're the ones the young engineers turn to, usually very quickly.

You may, or may not, care to be reminded that Ronald Reagan was sixty-nine when elected President of the United States. And there's a certain lady in Windsor, England, who turned eighty not so long ago and still maintains a punishing daily work schedule.

In the past fifty-four years this woman has received more than 3 million letters, hosted around 1.1 million guests at her famed garden parties, and made approaching 260 overseas visits to some 130 countries. She is a patron of more than 620 organizations and charities, and every day there is a full diary, with no two days ever the same.

And every Tuesday at 6.30 pm, the most powerful person in the land, the prime minister no less, comes calling to brief her on national and international events, and then to listen to her thoughts on affairs of state. Over the years, ten Prime Ministers, including Winston Churchill and Margaret Thatcher, have made this weekly pilgrimage. She is still everyone's favorite granny, despite the antics of a truly dysfunctional family, receiving 37,000 birthday cards and e-mails from around the world on her eightieth birthday.

And is there any talk of retirement? Most certainly not. The Queen of England does not retire. She just keeps going—receiving ambassadors, conferring honors, discussing affairs of state with the highest and the mightiest, accepting her lot as official opener of any building of note, visiting hospitals, and checking her stable of race horses. And if *she* can do it . . .

There's another breed that doesn't retire. Farmers. They just keep going, but every now and then they come up against an insurmountable barrier.

Bruce is what city folk always refer to as "the salt of the earth." By that they mean someone you can depend on, honest as the day is long, and not afraid of hard work. He was the fourth generation in his family to farm the area of land in the Australian state of New South Wales. Then the drought came, the worst in a hundred years.

They're well used to droughts in this barren land, but this one was different. It didn't last for months, it lasted for years. Bruce did what all farmers do; he borrowed from the bank to feed his stock, to keep them alive. As the drought dragged on, he borrowed more and more, until finally the drought and interest payments proved an unbeatable team. With apologies to the well-known song: "Bruce fought the war, and the war won."

And when farmers lose, they lose everything. Not just their farms, but their homes, livelihood, pension, community, everything. The effect is devastating. A man in his late fifties, Bruce began talking of retiring on a taxpayer handout. Not for long though—the farmer in him saw to that. What Bruce hadn't lost was his drive to survive. His genetic lifejacket saved him from drowning in what could easily have been a sea of depression.

The first and smartest thing he did was recognize he couldn't beat the bank and the drought on his own. He was doubly lucky, as his state government goes out of its way to protect farmers in such strife, with the Rural Assistance Authority providing a sympathetic service. With this assistance, Bruce was able to hold dignified discussions with his bankers and arrange an exit strategy that suited both parties. The plan enabled him to retain his key breeding stock and graze them on leased land while Bruce set about putting his life back together.

Certainly, he and his family were now living in a much smaller home, and the children were in a local school rather than at a private boarding establishment. It took courage and determination, but despite the loss of income and status, there was no loss of dignity.

With his prime breeding stock secured, Bruce began hiring himself out to other farmers, using their equipment. Within six months he had his own tractor, and a further eighteen months later he was an established farm contractor with a team of specialist workers and a flourishing business.

Three years on and his children are back in boarding school; he's working on a plan to buy back the family farm and any thought of retirement is long gone.

You should see the prospect of retirement as your own crisis, the equivalent of a personal drought and crippling bank loan and ask, "Am I going to surrender? Am I going to give up? "Am I going to climb up on the sledge?"

There are countless lists of tips on how to live a happy retired life. Some are common sense — loving relationships, exercise, fresh fruit, and clean water, right down to regular flossing, and not smoking — but it doesn't end there. People make a living writing these lists. They usually advise you to take up gardening and enjoy the simple things, with the subtext that that's all you're going to be able to afford. There's no end of advice out there on savings plans, pension schemes, and retirement homes. And what do all these messages have in common? Fear.

They're shock tactics designed to make you fearful about your future and convince you to put your faith, and money, with someone else who will look after it for you. The sole intention is to remove your independent thought processes and have you buy into the retirement nightmare that only "they" can help you with.

And that's the truly scary bit. All these people wanting to help you abdicate from life and hand over control to the youngsters who know better. Remember what we've been saying all along: these people want you to buy into the myth that as you reach a certain age everything will change. Well of course it will—if you let it. It'll become a self-fulfilling prophecy, and *you* will fulfil it.

We're reminded here of Jim, a hugely successful dog breeder who had one dream: to win the national championship. He used to tell his friends that his perfect scenario would be to have the winner's cup in one hand, his dog in the other and then drop dead. Sadly, when the day came and he did win the coveted prize, Jim suffered a massive heart attack at his moment of glory. Never underestimate the power of your mind to deliver exactly what you wish for.

> Never underestimate the power of your mind to deliver exactly what you wish for.

Remember when you were little and a month seemed so important? No one was ever just four years old. It was always four-and-a-half or soon-to-be-five. As teenagers we were forever explaining how we would soon be sixteen or eighteen. We did this because they were rites of passage. And then we stopped because we were adults.

So what is it with the nonsense that suddenly we have to become childlike again as we hit our sixties? Why should we suddenly accept the judgment of those younger than ourselves that we're past it and should sit back and enjoy what time we have left? It isn't going to happen. We're going to keep on living and start doing all the things we've been putting off for later. No more of that "if only . . ."

> Why should we suddenly accept the judgement of those younger than ourselves that we're past it and should sit back and enjoy what time we have left?

And if you do this, you'll start to manage your time more sensibly and have more of a life. Here's what life will be like if you do just that.

You are now a free person. And you've done it yourself, because you've realized you're the only person who *can* do it. Your friends will say you're lucky, but they're wrong. There's no luck in it—you're just smart, and certainly smarter than they are.

You have no intention of quitting at sixty-five or sixty or even fifty-five and burying yourself in some "wasteland." For inspiration, think of the class of 1946—Bill Clinton,

Cher, other vibrant people you know who are fully alive and turning sixty and ask why you would want to be different.

If there's a good reason why you can't carry on doing what you're doing, then think of a career change. That could mean making the tea down at the charity shop, nothing wrong with that, but you could also be thinking of a lucrative career change.

Remember, your imagination is a preview of your life to come. Use it for your own benefit. Imagine something wonderful, put a time frame around it, then just get on with it. Nike hit the nail on the head with its slogan — "Just do it."

> An alternative to retiring may be just slowing down, working smarter, not harder.

An alternative to retiring may be just slowing down, working smarter, not harder. Just remember the old huskies and no getting up on that sledge!

Key points to remember

✓ You're only old when you decide you are

✓ Think young, stay young

✓ Never underestimate the power of your mind to deliver what you wish for

✓ Keep on living and start doing all the things you've been putting off

20

The end is not nigh

You arrived in this world with a backpack containing the essentials of life, equipped with a host of abilities and talents that have served you well. So what on earth is stopping you from making all of those experiences continue to work for you both now and in the future? Once you recognize that your backpack is still overflowing with valuable assets, you can get on with living and plan for the future. Because life *is* simple. It starts out that way and then we grow up and make it unbelievably complicated. So how do we make the complex simple again?

You've decided not to retire but can't keep working in your present job. What should you do now? This is a very good question that cuts to the very heart of everything we're talking about and the financial reality for many of us.

Let's take you through the basics

To reiterate the basic principles: You arrived with your survival backpack full, genetically coded, and geared to prosper and survive. Your instinct for survival has been refined by evolution over millions of years and is fully primed to act as your guide and tell you whether the path you choose is safe or not. People often refer to this phenomenon as "gut instinct" or a "hunch." Sadly we've learned to override our better judgement, otherwise known as our intuition, usually to our cost.

Let us remind you yet again: your intuition is a "sacred gift," the most precious possession you'll ever have. It is unique to you, and is your single most powerful tool. Practice using it and you'll soon find it's invaluable. There are countless stories of people who've made costly decisions against their "better judgment" and now wish they'd listened to themselves.

The other secret is that everything we need is in our *own* backpack, not someone else's. Most of us tend to ignore our own gifts and insights and go searching for someone else to provide solutions and give us answers—indeed, we're actively encouraged to do so by a plethora of people and organisations offering to solve our problems for us.

Their pitch goes usually something like this: "Concerned about retiring? Buy a franchise, make money for life. Invest with us, in shares, property, futures, commodities—you name it, we have it." The world is alive with consultants and soothsayers, the majority saying, "Do as I say," not, "Do as I do."

So back to our original question: how do you avoid retirement? What do you do? It's as simple as ABC.

A Attitude
B Belief
C Courage

First you need the mental and moral disposition to want to make the change. Then you need to believe you can do it, and last of all you need the courage to get on

> Have the courage to get on with it—"Just do it."

with it—"Just do it." The good news is you already have all these attributes right there in your backpack, just waiting to be used.

So how does this get you a new job, or out of your current one? Think of yourself as a cruise missile. Set your target, marshal your resources and stay focused on your goal. See any setback as a normal correction, make the correction and continue.

> Think of yourself as a cruise missile. Set your target, marshal your resources and stay focused on your goal.

Cruise missiles don't travel in a straight line, they wobble all over the place, left and right, up and down, just like the decision-making process of the average human being. And, just like you, they have an inboard computer. Each time the missile moves off course—up, down, left or right—the computer makes an adjustment to bring it back. Occasionally it may overcorrect, requiring constant adjustment until the missile finally reaches its target.

That's exactly what your inboard computer will do for you. And your inboard computer, your intuition, is a million times more capable than any missile computer. It's fantastic, it's uniquely programmed just for you and it's free. All you have to do is use it. And because it was designed specifically with you in mind, don't let anyone else near the controls.

You are a unique, individual creation—the who or how of it doesn't much matter for the sake of our argument. What counts is that you arrived in this world equipped with a host of abilities and talents. While we don't always know why, most of us are better at some things than we are at others. Where you're sitting right now is most probably the result of a combination of latent talent, skill, hard work, and occasional luck. You are who you are as the result of your experience. So what on Earth is stopping you from using all that experience to work for you now and in the future? Fear.

Remember what we said before—fear is the shadow of safety, and it's the driver being used by all those people who want to make our decisions for us, and tell us how to live the rest of our lives. All you need to do is refuse. Take back the power. It really is that simple.

> Take back the power. It really is that simple.

And if you hear the doomsayers and the pessimists start preaching about the end being nigh, remember the end is irrelevant; what is important is to live life to the full, every day. Declare to the world, "I'm not here to live a little and then give up. I'm here to live every step of the journey," and there'll be no stopping you.

We set out to write a book geared to change the lives of all who read it, by identifying the retirement virus and demonstrating it can be deleted. We want to explode the myth of retirement because we strongly believe that no one should retire. No one should *want* to retire.

We accept that eventually each and every one of us will want to slow down and perhaps even take down our shingle and call it quits at the workplace. Yes, we may need to rearrange our lives to suit changing circumstances and requirements, but there's no room for the view that we should therefore stop working and vegetate.

And that's our point. You're *not* enslaved by continuing to live a useful and fruitful life; on the contrary, it's retirement and doing nothing that ultimately imprisons and disempowers you.

> It's retirement and doing nothing that ultimately imprisons and disempowers you.

If that still sounds a bit frightening, relax—you're not alone. Everyone else has been conditioned to believe that retirement is a natural progression, both your duty and your right. Well now you know retirement isn't natural, it's certainly no dream ending, so we're giving you permission to eliminate "retirement" from your vocabulary.

- ⌁ As of now you're going to keep on living.

- ⌁ As of now you'll manage your time, your money, and your life more sensibly.

- ⌁ As of now there'll be no more talk of "one day" taking a cruise, playing more golf, seeing more of the family, having time to relax, traveling, meeting up with friends, learning to paint, walking the Great Wall of China.

- ⌁ As of now there'll be no more talk of having to retire to get a life.

You're are going to do it all NOW and join the ranks of the truly successful people, the ones who can afford to retire, yet don't. Successful people love what they do because they have a passion, and a genuine passion never goes away, so they never stop.

21

You have the power

Do it. Just do it. No more buying into the fallacy that on a certain date you're off to the scrap heap, it's simply not true and flies in the face of your genetic heritage. You know the reality is quite the reverse, your whole reason for being revolves around a drive to be gainfully active. You also know it's never too late to avoid the retirement trap, and even if you have started down that path you can turn back.

> Your whole reason for being revolves around a drive to be gainfully active.

So keep your wits about you:

— Be extra positive and on guard against those misguided souls still preaching the retirement message.

— Ignore all those "financial advisors" trying to part you from your money—you don't need them because you're investing in your own future by staying fit and healthy and working.

— No more buying into the shock tactics designed to make you afraid, and into the fallacy that you have a sign stamped on your forehead that reads—"Best before sixty-five."

— No more accepting that the "best" of life has passed you by, nothing really matters any more, and nothing in life will be as good again. You know that's a load of rubbish and you have no intention whatsoever of sitting around in God's waiting room.

> Accept that the "best" of life has not passed you by.

— Carry on living well and plan your life and finances so you can continue to do so.

— Realize that times have changed, and retirement is a child of the past and no longer relevant in the twenty-first century where we recognize working as an integral part of life's purpose.

— We're not donkeys motivated by a carrot on the end of a stick.

— Remember, beneath all complexity lies simplicity.

The politicians may be warning that the entire pension scheme system will soon be bankrupt, but you don't care because it's no longer any concern of yours, you're too busy getting on with your life. You're listening to your intuitive brain as it hammers home the simple message, "Live: do anything you need do to be safe and survive." You're listening to your intuition, your unique and truthful sounding-board for what is right and wrong for *you*.

No more nonsense about buying a little car to "see you out" or plans to "move out" to "get away from it all." You're going to live where the action is and remain part of your community. No more doubts about vegetating and being useless either, because you can see a real future, with an action plan to live life to the fullest.

And you know you can do all of that because you've taken the power back and are in control of your own life, your own destiny. Retirement isn't going to destroy you, you're going to keep on living a worthwhile life. After all, retirement kills more people than hard work ever did. No one's going to hijack your brain and destroy your survival instinct. You understand, you may have to reorganize your life or change what you do or how you do it, but you're ready to accept the challenge. You won't be waiting for the government to ride to the rescue.

> Retirement isn't going to destroy you—you're going to keep on living a worthwhile life.

Never forget the definition of retirement: *to remove from view; withdraw from society*. And you have no intention of buying into that because you now understand the alternative to retiring can be as simple as slowing down and working smarter, not harder.

Your knowledge, experience, and skill make you hot property, and you'd be a fool to waste such fantastic assets by retiring. And you know there's a growing market out there for you as every developed economy seeks out older, experienced people to dig them out of the social and economic crisis they all face. You've been socially redefined as useful and productive, with your personal wealth including not only your material possessions but your mental and physical wellbeing.

> You're going to stay in the real world, surrounded by positive, lively people.

Best of all, by refusing to retire you've ensured financial security and independence for yourself. You're going to stay in the real world, surrounded by positive, lively people who're making a real contribution and getting on with the rest of their lives, while making plans and setting targets. You've replaced retirement with responsibility—responsibility for yourself.

> You've replaced retirement with responsibility— responsibility for yourself.

Of course you plan to up your body's maintenance program by taking care of the running repairs now, while you can best afford them. You're going to eat correctly, exercise, and sleep well, which you now know to be as important as a healthy diet and regular exercise. By getting seven-and-a-half or eight hours' sound sleep you'll see the difference as your productivity increases and your quality of life improves, all of which will make sure you're in the best possible shape to make the most of the years to come.

Now you're in charge, making decisions about the way your life will be lived. No more defeatist talk of retiring and making your way quietly to the final departure lounge. Now you have your drive back, along with the positive approach that drove you for so much of your life. You have no intention of jumping off the moving train or vegetating, you're much too busy planning for the future.

> You're in charge, making decisions about the way your life will be lived.

No more behaving like a victim or moping about what could have been—you've got the rest of your life to think about and it's time to start acting that way, like someone with a life ahead of them rather than a life behind them. It's time to start living your dreams, not waiting for some wish list to come true. No more, "if only . . ." and no more moaners and whiners. You're going to stay young at heart forever by thinking young, because, for you, sixty is the new forty.

The solution is so very simple: just keep working and living a joy-filled life and if, for whatever reason, you can't carry on doing what you're doing, then you'll find something else.

> For you, sixty is the new forty.

Go for it.
Right now.

You've learned your ABC and you have the Attitude, the Belief, and the Courage. And you're going to do it. Go for it. Right now.

What my retirement plans were

....

....

....

....

....

....

....

....

....

....

....

....

....

....

....

....

....

....

....

....

....

What I am going to do differently

....

....

....

....

....

....

....

....

....

....

....

....

....

....

....

....

....

....

....

....

....

....

What my
plans are now

....

....

....

....

....

....

....

....

....

....

....

....

....

....

....

....

....

....

....

....

How I'll put my
plans in place

....

....

....

....

....

....

....

....

....

....

....

....

....

....

....

....

....

....

....

....

....

*Beneath
all complexity
lies simplicity*